5 SMOOTH STONES

Leadership Lessons from the Life of King David

MARC BRISEBOIS

DEDICATION

To my beautiful wife Wendy. Patient, longsuffering and always loving through the many trials, challenges and blessings that have made up our journey together. Always ready to learn and grow, you have been a strength and encouragement to me. You are a true example of a Proverbs 31 woman. I could not have done any of this without you.

ACKNOWLEDGMENTS

Thank you to the people at Spruce Grove Community Church. They are a unique bunch of people in passion and love for God. Their willingness to flow with the move of the Holy Spirit to build a critical mass & foundation for the habitation of the Lord is something to behold.

Also many thanks to our proofreaders and copy editors including Wendy Brisebois, Jennifer Banas, Nicky Martineau, Ken Bitner, Michelle Noble and Laverne Kundert. And many thanks to a tireless worker and faithful administrative assistant, Brenda G. Smith, whose commitment and effort to each Watchman project has been full and consistent. Thank you all for your participation and being "all-in"!

ENDORSEMENTS

This book goes beyond the typical 'how to' approach to leadership striking at the true issues dividing good and bad leadership. It reveals and illuminates so many of the usual mistakes leaders make in their efforts. Balancing both truth with applicable examples, Marc demonstrates a clear grasp of the issues facing today's generation who are being trained for the Kingdom of God.

Wesley and Stacy Campbell
www.beahero.org
www.revivalnow.com
www.newlifechurch.bc.ca

In his new book, *'Five Smooth Stones-Leadership Lessons from the Life of King David'*, Marc Brisebois delights and challenges his readers with insights from his life-long study of successful leaders. You will find each paragraph filled with thought-provoking statements. Marc has a gift for succinctly capturing wisdom into memorable pictures and sayings. You will be glad you took the time to read this book. Your own leadership will be transformed by this important discussion about the place of character in ministry.

Richard Long
Together Canada
www.togethercanada.ca

I have always admired Marc Brisebois' revelation and wisdom regarding Kingdom truths and ability to effectively communicate them for the Body of Christ. I so appreciate Marc's focus on character as a centre point for effective leadership in this book *'Five Smooth Stones-Leadership Lessons from the Life of King David'*. Take, read, absorb and apply this revelation. Whether a leader of a few, or multitudes, the principles in this book will help you be all God has created you to be as a leader.

Faytene Grasseschi
Best Selling Author
Director of MY Canada and TheCRY Canada

Marc is writing to help us view leadership from a biblical perspective. This will ensure we as leaders do not bring harm by focusing on our position while ignoring conduct. For the past fifteen years I have often observed Marc gleaning from the wisdom of many Christian leaders, and now, coupled with that, he brings his own wealth of experience which has given him ample understanding and authority to speak on this important subject of leadership.

Rob Parker
Founding Director
National House of Prayer

What makes a good leader? Are they born or is it a learned skill? Read as Marc Brisebois reveals five secrets of outstanding leadership that King David possessed that made him a great leader even in the midst of unwise decisions. May this book encourage you to continue to be the leader that God is 'well pleased' with.

Rev. Dr. Margaret Court AO, MBE, PhdLLD(Hon)
Senior Pastor, Victory Life Centre
Perth, Western Australia

Marc is one of the few people I know who is able to take a few stones of biblical revelation and turn them into a monument of epic truth. Undoubtedly, this book will inspire and equip you to overcome impossible odds.

Michael A. Danforth
Mountain Top International

FOREWORD

We are living in precarious times – an age when godly values, morals and worldviews no longer guide personal and corporate culture. Society has gradually disregarded Biblical truth, absolutes no longer exist, and integrity is no longer esteemed.

In the following pages, Marc Brisebois powerfully paints an insightful and penetrating portrait of two kings, as he observes one who lives to gratify his own selfish desires, and another who builds his life on a solid foundation of faith and godly character.

The truths explored in *Five Smooth Stones – Leadership Lessons from the Life of King David*, will help you to understand that a leader – in fact, anyone desiring to impact others– must be a person whose life reflects God's nature. Timeless eternal realities emerge from the pages containing the power to transform your life. We cannot adjust the Word to fit society's changing value systems, nor can we expect those who follow us to be honest, selfless, loving and principled, if our own moral compass is distorted.

As Marc clearly portrays, character is not just a stream of external behaviors. It is an internal quality that emanates from a transformed mind. In spite of his failures and imperfections, God said of David, *"I have found David the son of Jesse, a man after my own heart, who will do all my will." (Acts 13:22 NKJV).* It should be the prayer of every person who reads this book, that God can say the same of them.

Bill Prankard
Bill Prankard Evangelistic Association
www.bpea.com

CONTENTS

INTRODUCTION

The presence or absence of real authoritative leadership is the pivotal issue on which rides the success of any enterprise. The excellence of the men or women at the helm of an organization be it government, a corporation or ministry will determine its ultimate capacity. The reasons by which one organization or even civilization rises in influence against another cannot be divorced from the collective quality of the people. Some will point to education and training as the chief ingredients for establishing a people but character is the ultimate litmus test of resolute strength. As a nation's character goes, so does its prosperity, status and influence.

Over the course of history great civilizations rise and fall. Today the stature of Western Civilization is diminishing. It has lost touch with the one element responsible for making it great: That is character. Character is the chief ingredient behind stable families and is a vital key in the making of great leaders. It may not be easily traceable but real character is found in a selflessness that can only emerge out of encounters with God. This is forged in a divine furnace accessible to those who hunger for truth.

When seen as mere behavior character can be copied or imitated. True 'god-likeness' is something else. It is a unique quality that cannot be replicated by man. Like life itself, it gives power to everything that moves, defining its beginning and end. As such, it is the mysterious x-factor behind every sustained venture and enterprise. Whether we are looking at a family, a business or an entire civilization, character born of our maker is an indispensible treasure.

The disappearance of character therefore declares the beginning of the end. The vacuum of leadership has begun to unfold in the western world and with it our ability to influence. The evidence is everywhere.

Some have erroneously believed the West has occupied this place of great influence as a matter of divine right. The reality is the bedrock success of the West is rooted in the knowledge of God. While that influence is presently eroding let it be understood that it rose on the wings of faith. The centrality of God and His Word in the hearts of people is what reforms a nation. The truth, loved and shared by a generation, gives rise to great leaders, which in turn creates great nations.

Going forward leadership will become an increasing catalyst for discussion and speculation. The marketplace desperately requires people of sufficient competence and substance. Given the right equations an actual dollar value could be affixed to the decline of character. Issues ranging from cost overrun due to absenteeism, internal theft, political corruption, and sickness related to reckless lifestyles, all go to tax the financial competitive power of our industries. The losses in efficiencies and productivity that so often can be traced to the kind emotional distraction usually absorbed by superior moral fiber. While these elements have always been hurdles for mankind they are increasing at an alarming rate.

As the cost of moral failure and fragmented character begin to be acknowledged and tallied, a great and desperate search for leaders will follow. It is a time of great opportunity for those who will embrace the true essentials of Biblical faith. Stable, honest, faithful men and women, will be worth their weight in gold.

I did not always understand the value of leaders. As a child I thought that being a leader was having the right to give orders but leadership is far more than this. It is an unavoidable dynamic of life even when there are no well defined structures. My initial ignorance of leadership has given way to a better understanding. It emerged very slowly; so slowly that I could not even point to a beginning.

I do remember being baffled by mentions of leadership where I could not see its relevance. Commentators would be talking about a hockey player's skills when out of nowhere they would mention the effect of a player's influence in the dressing room in terms of leadership. I dismissed the talk as irrelevant and thought once you became an adult, the world consisted of grown-ups doing what needed to be done. Each was self-sufficient, motivated and focused on doing their part in life. For me, it was only a matter of time before I would be part of the equation.

It is not clear to me where I got this idea but it might have been reinforced by movies. As I recall in the action 'flicks' of my childhood there was a great deal of gallantry. Men regularly stormed into danger! Whether it was John Wayne riding his trusty steed near a cliff edge to save the damsel in distress; a firefighter beating back ferocious flames to save a child from a burning building, or the man of war charging into battle without so much as a whisper of care, it all seemed too easy. Courage was so common I assumed it was part of being a grownup and how I longed to get there!

My enlightenment was gradual and a little shocking as I witnessed adults behaving like children. I discovered the world was not as I thought. *"How could this be?"* I thought. *"You are an adult"*. I could not understand this until I read the stories of Saul and David for in them I saw a child and an adult.

These accounts cemented in me something I could not have earlier imagined. Mainly that Saul though a "grownup", never actually emerged from childhood. So the qualities of leadership are not synonymous with age. Saul's tantrums were just one of the evidences of his immaturity. *"Then Saul cast a spear at him to kill him, by which Jonathan knew that it was determined by his father to kill David. ...Jonathan...was grieved for David, because his father had treated him shamefully" (1Samuel 20:33-34).* Desperately trying to act the part but never convincingly enough, Saul was a boy in a man's body. What was previously 'automatic' in my mind i.e. growing up, now offered no guarantees. There was a chance I could grow up and still remain a child. As I read about Saul I saw so much of myself in him. His fear and reluctance to lead reflected my own so much that I wondered whether I was destined to fail. It never dawned on me that the same insecurities and fears I struggled with plagued the larger part of the adult world as well. I vainly hoped the definition of being older meant these would be things of the past. I began a quest to make sure I did not remain as I was.

Offering a rod of hope was the life of David —a stark contrast to that of Saul. David's rule as king provides an outstanding legacy of great leadership. He began being a man when he was yet a boy. This was significant to my life as it created hope that I might be able to be like him. His most famous moment, the defeat of Goliath, is perhaps his most celebrated achievement. Countless sermons and Sunday school teachings amplify the drama of that fateful day yet it is not necessarily his greatest accomplishment. While it stands out clearly among the host of other significant conquests, one victory *'does not a dynasty create'*.

David became part of an enterprise with an enduring quality and the word legacy comes to mind. Many leaders, especially the politicians of our day, become very concerned with *'legacy'* in the twilight of their rule. They long to leave something enduring in the wake of their administrations as a memorial to themselves. Historically, leaders of the past have left architectural contributions, such as the Greek Pantheon or the Roman Coliseum. This desire partially exists because those who follow will rarely acknowledge the achievements of ones who have gone before them. It is especially uncommon to build on or *'carry on the legacy'* most particularly when they come from opposite ends of the political spectrum. The issue for the outgoing or aging leader becomes *'what can I build that has a sufficient ubiquitous quality that others will not tear down?'* What will have longevity? Through wisdom David was able to leave something that had longevity and quality but more importantly pleased God. In fact, God was so pleased that He continues to build on what David achieved. Now that is Legacy!

Of his colossal victory over Goliath what can be said? Standing in that field in defense of God was nothing short of miraculous. Equally unique was the courage to even step into battle in the first place. He stood at the precipice of destruction, figuratively carrying the honor of the entire nation in his hand. Literally, David held a sling and five smooth stones. *"Then he took his staff in his hand; and he chose for himself five smooth stones from the brook, and put them in a shepherd's bag, in a pouch which he had, and his sling was in his hand. And he drew near to the Philistine. "*(1 Samuel 17:40). He needed only one, but as king he would need much more than what one stone represented. The responsibility of leadership over a kingdom would require everything his training and upbringing could provide.

In this book I will look at 'five smooth stones', which are gems of wisdom and understanding. These are not the ones in David's hand when he fought Goliath, though they are no less significant. They represent the people and relationships that reveal at least five secrets of outstanding leadership. You will get a hint of the kind of man David was from the perspective of God.

1   THE FOUNDATION

David was anointed King by the prophet Samuel, but a vial of oil cannot win the respect of a nation. As David served under Saul it was said *"So David went out wherever Saul sent him, and behaved wisely. And Saul set him over the men of war, and he was accepted in the sight of all the people and also in the sight of Saul's servants"(1Samuel 18:5).* Proverbs tells us *"Through wisdom a house is built; and by understanding it is established; By knowledge the rooms are filled with all precious and pleasant riches"(Proverbs 24:3,4).*   True leadership is not defined by titles and privilege but by wisdom.

Building a Kingdom

David's battle with Goliath was a defining moment. It was a victory and a statement to the gods of the nations. Marking

the beginning of what was to follow: A legacy of countless
heroic acts, battles, victories and challenges which produced
the golden years of a dynasty declared to be ultimately
inherited by Jesus. The following is a prophetic declaration
concerning the Kingdom of God.

"Of the increase of His government and peace there will be no
end, upon the throne of David and over His kingdom, to order
it and establish it with judgment and justice from that time
forward, even forever. The zeal of the Lord of hosts will
perform this" (Isaiah 9:7).

The importance of David's life is probably most reflected in
the fact that Jesus would ultimately sit on the throne of
David. *"He will be great, and will be called the Son of the*
Highest; and the Lord God will give Him the throne of His
father David."(Luke 1:32). One should not underestimate the
importance of such an honor. Imagine the Creator of all
things is to receive an inheritance named after a man. This
suggests something of a superior and heavenly quality in what
David established. But what was it and how did it come
about? What kind of values did David operate in to create
something worthy of the Lord? What did David understand
that others did not? All these are questions we must ask and
have answered if we hope to contribute to the Kingdom of
God.

Who among us wants to live a life of perceived morality and
godliness only to find in the end, nothing we did increased the
Kingdom. Like David we have been called to bear fruit that

remains. The throne of David is now synonymous with the eternal reign of Jesus. David helped establish a throne that was worthy of the King of Kings and would last forever. When you are looking for something that will remain, 'forever' is a great quality. It is the kind of durability you cannot buy.

Clearly there was David's obvious faith and we know he was highly praised as being a man after God's own heart *"... The LORD has sought for Himself a man after His own heart, ..."(1 Samuel 13:14)*. Surely this is a key! But what does it mean to have a heart after God? We can only speculate, but if anything it must include loving the things which God loves.

God is always looking for those who will love what He loves. It is not unlike the relationship between an artisan and his apprentice. When a young apprentice goes to work, it is not simply to learn a skill; he is in fact developing a value system. Within this value system is the creation of a threshold of excellence. It has been said of some famous artists they could stare at a canvas for hours before adding one simple brush stroke. The result of that kind of patience is perfection; the catalyst for that kind of patience is a higher value system. If the apprentice does not absorb some dimension of that love of excellence he will inherit mere behaviors. He will not become an artisan, but rather a laborer with skills. During the training the artisan is answering for the apprentice the question of worth: What is worthy to keep and what is fit for the trash? It is a question of quality - **the greater the quality, the greater the value and the longer the existence.** This distinction is critical to the creation of valuable, timeless art.

As it relates to God it means appreciating the standards by which God builds. The house He is building is enduring! He is looking for what is in fact entirely timeless because He lives in eternity. Like an artisan of uncommon skill, He sees what mankind cannot see. He longs for a people who will allow themselves to be taught. He is looking for those willing to be stripped of their personal opinions and come alongside unquestionable genius in order to inherit His value system.

Like Little Children

As a kind Father, God will take us from glory to glory. When we are young and immature the only requirement is sincere desire. He appreciates any attempts toward His will. Like the mother posting her 5 year olds water colored portraits on the fridge, our Father values our meager contributions. This is not to say these efforts have crossed the threshold of actual usefulness, but at the very least, they represent a desire to please. This is a foundation on which God can build provided we are willing to move on from there.

In time, pictures on the fridge give way to meaningful contributions as our abilities evolve. The journey is long, sometimes frustrating and fraught with many pitfalls. A child, like an apprentice, can begin to think of their teacher as impossible and harsh. At this point, trust in the master's love is the only thing that will keep us committed to our training. In the end only those who are willing to receive His value system can participate in the building. Those who choose to love what He loves and despise what He despises can add value to this eternal structure–the Kingdom. This will become the point of God's evaluation as He surveys our contribution. Paul understood this when He warned of the dire consequences of building with inferior materials and expertise. Consider this:

"For no other foundation can anyone lay than that which is laid, which is Jesus Christ. Now if anyone builds on this foundation with gold, silver, precious stones, wood, hay, straw, each one's work will become clear; for the Day will declare it, because it will be revealed by fire; and the fire will test each one's work, of what sort it is." (1 Corinthians 3:11-13)

The Kingdom of God can only be built with suitable materials, anything less is worthless to Him. David's love for God's standard postured him to contribute in a unique way. Ultimately this was the secret of the Lord which David carried all the days of his life. He understood what God was after and yielded himself to His ways. Meditating on God's word, he allowed the excellence of God to be grafted into his being. *"… That I may live and keep Your word. Open my eyes, that I may see wondrous things from Your law. … Do not hide Your commandments from me. "(Psalm 119:17-19). "Blessed is the man Who walks not in the counsel of the ungodly, Nor stands in the path of sinners, Nor sits in the seat of the scornful; But his delight is in the law of the LORD, And in His law he meditates day and night. He shall be like a tree planted by the rivers of water that brings forth its fruit in its season, whose leaf also shall not wither; and whatever he does shall prosper." (Psalm 1:1-3).* David invited those ways to shape his attitudes and perceptions. Finally they dictated the manner in which David dealt with people.

The following reflects the heart of David for God's values.

- ❖ I will delight myself in Your statues; I will not forget your word. (Psalm 119:16)
- ❖ Your testimonies also are my delight. (Psalm 119:24)
- ❖ And I will walk at liberty, for I seek your precepts. (Psalm 119:45)
- ❖ My hands also I will lift up to Your commandments, which I love, and I will meditate on Your statutes. (Psalm 119:48)
- ❖ Unless Your law *had been* my delight, I would then have perished in my affliction. (Psalm 119:92)
- ❖ I will never forget Your precepts, for by them You have given me life. (Psalm 119:93)
- ❖ Oh, how I love Your law! It *is* my meditation all the day. You, through Your commandments, make me wiser than my enemies; For they *are* ever with me. I have more understanding than all my teachers, For Your testimonies *are* my meditation. I understand more than the ancients, Because I keep Your precepts. I have restrained my feet from every evil way, That I may keep Your word. ...(Psalm 119:97-101)
- ❖ Your testimonies are wonderful; Therefore my soul keeps them. The entrance of Your words gives light; It gives understanding to the simple. I opened my mouth and panted, For I longed for Your commandments. . . .(Psalm 119:129-131)
- ❖ My tongue shall speak of Your word, For all Your commandments *are* righteousness. Let Your hand become my help, For I have chosen Your precepts. I long for Your salvation, O LORD, And Your law *is* my delight. Let my soul live, and it shall praise You; And let Your judgments help me. I have gone astray like a lost sheep; Seek Your servant, For I do not forget Your commandments. (Psalm 119:172-176)

Each of these statements represent the cord of faith and trust leading David throughout his life. They gave him an ability to see and understand the secret mysteries of wisdom that in turn guided his steps. These subtle but powerful secrets, hidden in the fabric of David's history are the values which mirror the construct of the heavens. They are heavens present realities and the reason for their durable nature! Every decision, every action had purpose as defined by these values. These are the things David's contemporaries failed to recognize or appreciate because these realities did not originate from the earth. They are the definition of the enduring Kingdom now being unveiled in the earth. These are the realities which form the foundation for the kingdom that fell in the lap of Solomon. It is these same realities which made the throne of David suitable for the King of Kings.

2   THE THRESHOLD

The threshold is the difference between heaven and earth, temporal and eternal, flesh verses spirit. True spiritual leadership begins with seeing the great gulf dividing these realities. If we cannot distinguish between the temporal and the eternal, how then can we build? The construct of the Kingdom of God consists only of what emerges from the Spirit. Then, and only then, will it have the durable quality we require. It can be mimicked to create the identical appearance without actually being the same. Appearances mean nothing. In fact, the very process of our training in the Lord enables us to look past appearances. If we cannot see this, our work is already in jeopardy.

Leadership begins with acknowledging and taking responsibility for the building materials and those materials come from the secret places of our hearts. "The *heart is deceitful above all things, and desperately wicked; who can know it? I, the LORD, search the heart; I test the mind, even to give every man according to his ways, according to the fruit of his doings"(Jeremiah 17:9-10)*. We cannot escape what is in our heart by imitation or the parroting of appropriate slogans.

> **True faith is not in words from the mouth, but truth from the heart.**

It is all about the heart. Whether we know it or not, what is in our hearts becomes part of what we build. If there is pride in the heart of the leader, the building will contain the same. For example, when we speak on the theme of faith with fear in our heart, fear will be sown. The appearance of having faith will mean nothing!

I remember a few years ago sharing in a church on the theme of 'Entering the Rest of God'. The audience was comprised of some senior Christian leaders. Afterward, as we spoke, one of them commented saying *'it is difficult to share on rest when you are striving'*. Though the words and phrases were correct, my message contained an internal contradiction. I was unable to do what I was telling others they should do. This is the missing ingredient in much ministry today. We are saying the right things but the inverse comes out. While we might want to share on faith, we cannot if fear is in our heart.; at least we cannot to the degree that we fear. True faith is not in words from the mouth but truth from the heart.

Intimidation, control, and fear can be a part of every sermon, action or policy a leader puts forward. Whether or not those things are visible to the naked eye, they will appear somewhere in your building. Even if we are sincere, our sincerity is no defense. This is one of the reasons we are warned against promoting a novice. They have the outward behaviors well rehearsed, but it is a question of purity. No matter our intent, out of the heart come the issues of life (Proverbs 4:23).

Leaders who use such devices cannot build what is pure. Fear might produce obedience or unity in the short term, but it is not a unity from above, nor will it last. *"Do not be deceived, God is not mocked; for whatever a man sows, that he will also reap" (Galatians 6:7).* For this reason Paul warned leaders to be careful how they build.

"For no other foundation can anyone lay than that which is laid, which is Jesus Christ." *(1 Corinthians 3:11)*

A wise master builder pays special attention to his building materials. When the materials are sub-par so is the building. We are meant to build with heavenly materials void of human strength. Unfortunately, these are not easily found. Many build presumptuously thinking appearance is the same as substance. Who among us has purchased cheap knock-offs only to later discover the lack of quality? The difficulty is that quality materials are impossible to distinguish from inferior materials unless the Chief Artisan has imparted to you His threshold of excellence.

It is one thing to emulate behavior; it is another to move from the same heart. In our quest to do something for Jesus, the result is often a form of godliness void of heaven's power. David was a man who moved with an understanding of the ways of God. His example has inspired many to follow him and celebrate his achievements. Whereas it is easy to notice the faith and courage of a David, less noticeable are the secrets or mysteries of wisdom, which actually produce an enduring kingdom. While we cannot undervalue the contribution of the obviously great moments, it is perhaps the quiet moments which speak with greater volume.

The Quiet Moments

What and where are these moments? They are everywhere, but are most clearly revealed in relationships. While most people talk of 'what' David did and said, the secret is always in the 'why', David 'did' and 'said'.

The chronology of the kings of Israel is not necessarily a teaching but a story of lives lived out in public. You will not find a book or a poem itemizing the 10 principles by which David governed and there is no book of 'David's Motivations'. Still, we can understand a great deal about a man's attitudes and beliefs by the way he interacted with others. Obscured by the details of emotion and drama are golden nuggets of truth. These truths form the heart of the work we do in the name of the Lord.

In David's life they can be seen in the way he related to people around him. In some cases it is not what the relationships did but what they did not do. At other times it was David's response to the people in the relationships with him. Regardless, each gives a peek into the kind of material God uses to build.

3   DAVID AND JONATHAN
(AS SEEN THROUGH THE EYES OF SAUL)

Significant among David's relationships was the one he had with Jonathan, the son of Saul. The affection and mutual respect between them was profound and costly. Jonathan, as the first born of King Saul, was the rightful heir to the throne of Israel. Yet he was willing to pursue a relationship with David knowing the potential threat to his inheritance. His obvious readiness to lose this place of privilege to his friend is astounding. It testifies to the incredible respect he had for David. For us it begs the question—what kind of man deserves this kind of respect. The answer is neither simple nor brief. The truth is that the example of David will give us insight into the very meaning of the word Leadership.

True Relationship

Chronicling the anatomy of David and Jonathan's relationship would be a tedious affair. Further complicating the issue is the absence of details. The scriptural narrative is not like a novel where the development of personalities and relationships is central to the writing. We do not see descriptive explanations of David and Jonathan's bonding. However, if you have even a cursory knowledge of this part of scripture you are keenly aware of the depth of their connection. Saul himself, in a condemning & explosive rage summarizes their commitment to one another: *"Then Saul's anger was aroused against Jonathan, and he said to him, "You son of a perverse, rebellious woman! Do I not know that you have chosen the son of Jesse to your own shame and to the shame of your mother's nakedness? For as long as the son of Jesse lives on the earth, you shall not be established, nor your kingdom. Now therefore, send and bring him to me, for he shall surely die" (1 Samuel 20:30-31).*

Jonathan is not naïve, but appears so to Saul. *"And Jonathan answered Saul his father, and said to him, "Why should he be killed? What has he done?"(1 Samuel 20:32).* In that moment *"... Saul cast a spear at him to kill him, by which Jonathan knew that it was determined by his father to kill David."(1 Samuel 20:33).* Jonathan rises stunned and angry with his father. *"So Jonathan arose from the table in fierce anger, and ate no food the second day of the month, for he was grieved for David, because his father had treated him shamefully." (1 Samuel 20:34).* Jonathan was willing to accept the consequences of his friendship with David. He understood that he was in fact choosing to forgo his rule in favor of David. Jonathan had such a love and respect for David that it made him deaf to the tormenting voices in Saul's head.

David's commitment and love toward Jonathan was mutual and he declared their love as being more significant than the love of women. *"I am distressed for you, my brother Jonathan; you have been very pleasant to me; your love to me was wonderful, surpassing the love of women" (2 Samuel 1:26).* It is a monument to covenant, a bond able to endure the most extreme of consequences.

Artificial Relationship

The relationship between Jonathan and David is a thing of beauty and it provides for us a measure. Great love and sacrifice create a contrast by which selfishness is suddenly very obvious. The bond between these men highlights a missing dimension, a conspicuous absence of any meaningful relationship in the life of Saul.

Nowhere do we see Saul relating to anyone in a manner that would reveal his personal side. In the tale of Saul's life there is much about his role as the rising underdog and his regrettable reign as king over Israel, but there is a woeful barrenness in the area of relationship. Once he became king his posture was always one of leader to follower. His position and title came to define him as a person. This is not uncommon for men and women in authority!

This tendency, the need to hide behind position, points to an inner weakness. It may emerge as an effort to solidify our standing but it can limit our influence as a leader. Relationships are complex and they are tricky things to navigate. They require compromise and the ability to give and take. Fear and insecurity on the other hand create a compelling need to control. They demand circumstances that do not challenge or deviate from expectations. Asserting dominance is the chief way we acquire control, thus, a position gives us the potential for dominance without the messiness of relationship. It is simply easier to bark orders or cut off heads than it is to gain people's respect through tedious things like stable love and faithfulness.

Fear and insecurity do more than rob us of our joy and capacity for relationship. They are taskmasters whose aim is our ultimate destruction. When we are driven to continually master others, there is no room for letting down our guard. The substitute for real relationship is a posture where I am always dominant and live through my position. But it is an exhausting exercise, impossible to maintain with any degree of regularity. Those who live this way remind me of scenes from the Star Trek sci-fi television program. The Enterprise would be under attack until their shields would begin to fail. At the moment of crisis Captain Kirk would tell them to *'divert life support systems to the forward shield'*. You cannot sustain this scenario for long. Likewise, it is impossible to maintain a constant competitive and defensive posture. Saul could not live that way either and eventually crumbled from the inside out.

Saul was in effect delaying the inevitable. In his quest for respect he hid behind a title. When leaders find themselves in a preeminent position, it is easier to keep functioning from this one dimension: 'Leader to follower'. Saul was clearly more comfortable with this kind of arrangement as it ensured that he would always have the upper hand.

There is a certain comfort with this kind of order; the road of least resistance. For David it was not an option to regress to artificial relationships. He discovered the freedom available in being 'himself'. Real relationships are a kind of emancipation, releasing the driving spirit behind control. To those who have tasted them, real relationships are far too satisfying to be exchanged for tyranny of the false! Saul was willing to compromise for the sake of his internal safety where dominance took the guesswork out of the equation.

This is one of the reasons men in authority struggle at home with their spouses. At work they are rarely questioned and their position is secure and defined by a corporate hierarchy. In that context there are clear rules, procedures and protocols. As heads of departments, foremen, and CEO's, the ability to use coercion(e.g. threats of dismissal) helps maintain order. At home they are forced to draw upon other attributes to lead and these often go undeveloped in favor of the easier road.

Roles that give us clear-cut lines of behavior make relationships superfluous. We don't have to develop the skills necessary for deep bonds, because corporate culture dictates to us what we should do. Over time and without the benefit of actual relationship, our ability to be real disappears. In the end we know how to behave toward people in authority and can always teach and lead those beneath us, but we lose the ability to craft new genuine affiliation without our artificial tutor. When forced into a dynamic that rests on our abilities as human beings we malfunction and this is where David shows his capacity as a leader. He forged his relationships in a vacuum without the benefit of political position or privilege. David's ability to create deep bonds with both his peers in the wilderness and Jonathan at the king's table points to a profound ability worth pursuing. It was within Saul's power to make the same choices, but he did not.

Insecurity

If we wish to be the kind of leader that David was we must explore and remove the roots of our own insecurities. Insecurity is but one reason for the lack of intimacy in a relationship. In peer relationships authority issues are not spelled out, in other words, nobody says 'you are in charge'. When dealing with friends you lead by the nature of who you are on the inside. If you have nothing inside, you have nothing with which to lead. Intimacy is therefore terrifying! Intimacy in the life of a leader can be a barometer. It is a reflection of the actual strength of a leader and by this measure Saul, though physically imposing, was no match for David, or Jonathan.

Saul was a man with outward stature but without inward power. He was said to be *'little in his own eyes'*. As such he lived a life of hiding and pretense. On the day of his inauguration, for example, he was found hiding in the equipment *"When he had caused the tribe of Benjamin to come near by their families, the family of Matri was chosen. And Saul the son of Kish was chosen. But when they sought him, he could not be found. Therefore they inquired of the LORD further, "Has the man come here yet?" And the LORD answered, "There he is, hidden among the equipment"* (1 Samuel 10:21, 22). His 'flight response' to the calling of the Lord can tell us something of what was at the core of his being. He was insecure and hesitant, requiring constant encouragement from Samuel. Some may see this hesitation as something to be praised. In other circumstances that may well have been true, but for Saul it was a dangerous kind of insecurity.

Insecurity ought not to be mistaken as humility. Insecurity fears being in the public eye, whereas humility does not require it. This is why we saw Saul run from the responsibility of public office. Humility can compliment and celebrate ability; it simply acknowledges where it came from. *"Every good gift and every perfect gift is from above, and comes down from the Father of lights, with whom there is no variation or shadow of turning"* (James 1:17). Insecurity blushes at recognition. It blushes because it is in fact reveling in the moment but believes it ought not. It is as a sign that it cannot help but take the credit. It both shuns and desperately wants acknowledgement.

Insecurity has no confidence, therefore does not rise up with ambition. However, it actually would love to dominate and if it doesn't, it is because it does not believe it has the ability to do so. With the necessary encouragement insecurity will take the reins with a vindictive and cruel aggression, ready to crush anything remotely threatening.

Insecurity is simply the inverted face of pride and self-exaltation. It is a face that pivots from one side to the other based on environment. It has chameleon-like qualities, always avoiding detection by concealing its true nature. Without position and endorsement it is reserved and unassuming. In the face of public approval it is tyrannical and oppressive. This defines the life of Saul but is the antithesis of what we see in the relationship between David and Jonathan.

Breaking Insecurity

Some years ago I was invited to be part of a group that would meet in a home twice a week. The goal was simple: Reality and Intimacy. The idea put forward was that we couldn't be more intimate with God than we were with people. This should ring true since Jesus told us *"... 'Assuredly, I say to you, inasmuch as you did it to one of the least of these My brethren, you did it to Me.'" (Matthew 25:40)*

The meeting was not very well structured and was attended by a wide variety of people. There were different generations as well as races represented. The format was simple and each meeting began with a bit of worship. After a time the leader (a friend and ministry associate) would open his heart to give us a glimpse into 'who he was' by detailing things he presently struggled with. He shared about fears he was trying to overcome and issues of tension in his closest family relationships.

The effect upon my heart was remarkable as I knew this person to be an anointed man of God. To me he represented a quality of leader, and walked in a favor of God, that I could only aspire to. When he shared his personal frustration with himself, my heart was relieved. I thought, *'if you struggle with these things and God has anointed you, then I do not have to fear being rejected by God myself'*.

The truth is I had begun to believe a lie. The lie told me the secret behind the favor God in my life was related to my performance. I had begun to believe that it was my 'perfection' or 'notion of perfection' that was responsible for the ministry anointing. Of course I had rationalized this thinking on the basis of the need for 'purity'. Not realizing the conflict growing inside of me as the power of shame insidiously increased. It propelled me into a kind of hiding, hoping somehow these issues would mysteriously vanish. They were not huge sins but they were secret flaws responsible for a growing tide of torment. Each time my friend boldly revealed his imperfection it pierced the invisible stronghold of fear within me. With no effort on my part I was being released each time he shared about his imperfection. It was then that I began to see the power sustaining my imperfections were not the imperfections themselves, but the fear of discovery and disqualification.

After he shared he would then give opportunity for others to be real and vulnerable. It brought a kind of deep freedom as each held on to secrets they feared would diminish and disqualify them before others and God. All around the room hidden veils of secrecy were being lowered, creating a sense that we were for the first time truly seeing one another. The net effect was an intimacy beyond comprehension. At the conclusion of those three months, we felt like we had known each other our entire lives. It was the kind of bond you felt with childhood friends or what men in war must feel with each other. It was then that I understood the secret of Paul's authority and freedom- he was not afraid to embrace his weakness. The choice we are given is to either hide our weaknesses or expose them. When we are exposed they lose their power over us. This is what David discovered but Saul did not.

Conclusion

Leadership is a craft much the same as public speaking or writing. Good leaders are the result of years of development. David's experience in close quartered surroundings allowed his flaws and weaknesses to come to light. For us to continue to grow and develop, we need an atmosphere of accountability. We need people to whom we can reveal our deepest fears and disappointments; people who will speak freely and honestly concerning their own lives, and their perceptions of ours. We are called to work out our salvation with fear and trembling. Leadership will often mean showing others your fear and trembling, while steadfastly walking in obedience.

4 LEADERSHIP TODAY

Some time ago I watched an interview by a political reporter who was contrasting the leadership styles of two Canadian Prime Ministers. One was wildly successful; the other had a decent run, but was largely considered an inferior leader. After throwing out a variety of comparisons between their styles, politics, and constituencies, the astute reporter summarized their differences in the most poignant manner. He said that the superior leader simply did not care what anyone thought of him. The other desperately wanted to be liked. The need to have popular appeal brings leaders into servitude – the posture of following. The obvious problem is that one cannot lead when they are following.

The same issue continues to tempt and try potential leaders today as it did with David & Saul. Leaders who need to be liked are easily manipulated. This is because the 'need to be liked' translates to a fear of being disliked. Fear is a tyrant however. It is a compelling force responsible for so many unhealthy policies.   This is why insecure men and women in positions of power become the worst of leaders. Once an insecure leader comes into prominence they cannot let it go. Position becomes the ultimate endorsement. Left unchecked they eventually employ any means to maintain their position. Like their own master (fear), they will become tyrants.

This scenario does not have to look like a banana republic, or so many of the brutal dictatorships. They can exist quietly in the most sterile of environments. Fear can be a quiet seducer, like mold growing in some dark secret place; hidden but poisoning everything. Fear coins practices whose only goal is sustained influence. These practices become so common place that we barely acknowledge them. When the next generation learns to accept and employ the same practices. One of the most widespread and accepted practices comes out of the erroneous belief that i*n order for a leader to maintain respect he cannot be close or vulnerable to those he seeks to lead.*

The problem with debugging this, dare we call it *'leadership principle',* is that it can work for a period of time. There is power in maintaining an air of secrecy through separation. The shadowy mystique that comes with the illusive personality creates interest and intrigue. For the popular leader this is a problem and they will do what they can to hide their more human qualities. Because their appeal and authority rests in attracting the approval of the greatest number of people, their bent is to create distance between their public and private image. The only solution is–*become all things to all people by being nothing except what they expect.* Followers never get to see them as another human being. This creates a certain allure, leading to a form of respect, or even awe. For the insecure leader it provides leverage in the fight, however, it also binds them to an increasingly arduous course. Once one has given into the urge to appear better than others, there is no end to the tyranny which follows. When you build a following on the false premise of 'superiority' and encourage people to believe what is false, there can remain only the certainty of inevitable collapse. This path leads to increasing deception, confusion and, given time, literal madness.

Truth & Transparency

In looking for qualities of true leadership, we must ask how do real leaders conduct themselves? What does one do in the face of personal weakness? We must allow ourselves both time and space to develop. I remember hearing someone once say *'Premature authority leads to superficiality'*. This is why intimacy is impossible for the weak leader. He has been thrown into a role he cannot fulfill and therefore is compelled to conceal who he really is. If he does not have the courage to be himself he must embrace superficiality.

David lived in the most open and intimate way without ever losing his power to lead. Saul, however, was a very poor leader, so his only option was to conceal. To be completely fair the opportunity to develop was never given to him; without notice he was thrust into the limelight of leadership without training or development. From a human standpoint he probably did his very best, but the fact remains Saul was not a good leader and David became a great one.

David grew progressively in wisdom and authority through various trials, struggles and stages of leadership. The foundation of his life rested on this point: David was secure because he knew who he was. In his worship he drew near to the Lord. One of the by-products of drawing near is you hear Him tell you who you are. This imparts the essence of security and root of genuine authority. One cannot hope to be a great leader without this foundation.

From this foundation point David had opportunity to develop and he made the most of every challenge. Jonathan's respect for David was not on account of some awesome perfection. It was because David navigated these challenges with integrity and humility. The best leaders are not perfect leaders; they are individuals who inspire by virtue of their honest perception of their successes and failures. Such an individual will have an amazing ability to illicit confidence and devotion from those who follow him. David's honesty of heart and willingness to humble himself before man and God displayed an unpretentious soul.

An insecure man is not able to admit failure. He is too eager to impress and not likely to accept the truth concerning his own weakness. In addition, he will be intolerant of others who err. He will reserve a level of scorn for any who detect his flaws, and/or those who mistakenly try to help by showing him the error of his ways. The motivation of this man's heart will be to protect his image by denying any weakness and by keeping at arms distance anyone who threatens to expose or remind him of his state. Saul was such a man and could not command the respect of those closest to him. This forced him down a destructive road of denial, pretense and increasing frustration as the objects of his ambitions fell from his grasp.

David's Accomplishments

Part of David's advantage was the opportunity to develop in more obscure surroundings. He grew in secret, away from the eyes of the nation. Growing with him were men who would later become heroes and giants in Hebrew history. *"And everyone who was in distress, everyone who was in debt, and everyone who was discontented gathered to him. So he became captain over them. And there were about four hundred men with him"(1 Samuel 22:2).* Initially, these men were not known for their loyalty, honor or integrity. They had somehow become discontent with the system and they were actually far less likely to trust another authority figure.

This type of follower is the one that will truly test the mettle of a leader. They are leery of the ambitions of leaders and tend to impose resentment from their past onto present leaders. They are quick to rebel and quick to think of you as just another ambitious person climbing the ladder of success.

Through leading these men, David was thrust into an environment of serious accountability. Every move he made was under scrutiny and there was no hiding. As he and his men were forced into caves or whatever base accommodations were available, there was no room for privacy. In this environment everything about you becomes public knowledge and the accountability becomes even tighter. David was prevented from living apart from his men ensuring they 'knew' him, weaknesses and all. Unlike Saul, David was unable to choose the privilege of royalty, that is living at arm's length from his men, separated by protocols, luxurious courts and ivory towers. He never had the opportunity to create boundaries between himself and those around him.

The primitive circumstances coupled with his love of the truth enabled David to look squarely at himself. Faced with his flaws, he lived a life of evolution–constant change and advancement were the outcome. To his credit he took the opportunities for change as they were offered him, both in secret and in public. Even so, he stumbled only to recover (2 Samuel 11). When he sinned with Bathsheba he first tried to cover it up but God's accountability overtook him. Eventually he embraced correction and rebuke openly. Saul, for fear of losing his place of veneration, would allow no intimacy except that which he could control and regulate.

> *The tendency in our journey as believers is to take a shortcut through transformation. This kind of attempt will always be met with frustration.*

The book of James says, *"For where envy and self-seeking exist, confusion and every evil thing are there"(James 3:16).* This was Saul, a man driven by fear and ambition, but collapsing on the inside. This kind of man depends on outward appearances, beautiful clothes and surroundings to tell him he is king, but he is a man with a confused identity. We see Saul as a miserable soul desperately seeking a sense of worth through the acclaim of man. The harder he sought it the more anxious and desperate he became. Trying to be something we are not is always an uphill battle and eventually the energy needed to maintain the illusion will run dry and the life we created will come crashing down around us. Like the false refurbished front on a dilapidated building, the real problem is still behind the veneer.

What really lies beneath the surface of a fabricated life? The answer is unimaginable paranoia, which begs not to be found out or disturbed. It is a raging lunacy, which covets the reality others might have and yet detests them at the same time. In some quarters of the Church it is the only model provided and it is false. The fruit of it will always be confusion and failure.

Earthen Vessels

The tendency in our journey as believers is to take a shortcut through transformation. This kind of attempt will always be met with frustration. Picture the impatient driver at rush hour looking for a faster way. They will inevitably run into another bottleneck. The kind of transformation we need cannot happen by skipping ahead of the queue. The process determines the destination and we must be patient. The integrity of the process is critical to the transformation.

The real outcome is something we call 'glory in earthen vessels'. When we are born-again, God has put His glory in us. He has sown into us a tremendous power which comes from the glory of the knowledge of Jesus. As it is written, *"For it is the God who commanded light to shine out of darkness, who has shone in our hearts to give the light of the knowledge of the glory of God in the face of Jesus Christ. But we have this treasure in earthen vessels, that the excellence of the power may be of God and not of us" (2 Corinthians 4:6-7).*

God has done this in order to change us. It is a glorious thing but He put it in 'earthen vessels'. Our tendency is to want to make the earthen vessel glorious; unfortunately this is not what God promised. In fact it is the exact inverse of what we are meant to do and be. We are not meant to make the vessel glorious but to house the glory in a very humble and unimpressive earthen vessel. When we attempt the alternate we fight against God. The Kingdom starts from the inside while human strength starts from the outside. The horrible truth is that no amount of human strength can change the fallen nature of man: it can only conceal it. The postures of these two approaches are diametrically opposed to one another.

I once served with a man in ministry who seemed quite competent as a leader. He had just returned from visiting his family in another part of the country and was disheartened by their response to him. I enquired as to what great evil had been done to him and he responded by telling me they did not honor him as the man of God. His words were *to them I was just their brother—good old Peter*. He was disheartened because he believed his position as a minister would command the respect his character could not. His disappointment came from an erroneous belief.

The answer for him and other leaders is 'be content to be yourself'. Your sphere of respect should increase quite naturally as you increase. Inward changes for good will always be reflected in obvious outward change. These changes will become the foundation of your influence and authority. When you attempt to advance past your actual condition, God will allow people to remind you just who you are. If we become disheartened or angry at these reminders, we are lying to ourselves. Saul hated the reminders and sought to silence them at any cost.

David's lack of self-consciousness and easygoing confidence were attributes Saul both coveted and detested. That is why he became the scapegoat of Saul's lost ambitions. His presence ignited a desperate rage, which became increasingly irrational. Unaware of the growing scorn in Saul, David went about casually living his life. He simply served faithfully, using every circumstance as an opportunity for change and growth. For Saul, there could be no growth because there could be no transparent vulnerable relationships; the exposure they required was quite impossible. All energy was focused on the job of projecting the illusion of success. Inside the masterfully decorated shell is a withering shadow of the exterior, no longer fit for any authority or position. How are you doing

Saul? The answer always is and must be: *'On top and rising'*. As you will see, a humble and free disposition enables reconciliation and peace in the most adverse of circumstance.

5   DAVID AND ABNER

Leadership requires various people skills. We are not talking about manipulating or coercing people, instead we refer to the kind of character traits synonymous with the New Testament believer. Among those traits is the ability to forgive and restore relationship. Petty, self-centered people can never function far beyond a limited personal agenda. They are forever caught in the vortex of their own tragedies, imprisoned by whatever 'injustices' befall them. In David's dealings with Abner he demonstrated what it meant to forgive and overcome,   thus highlighting the power of a kingdom vision. Somehow, even though he was a victim, he rose above personal vendettas to do what was right for the nation. One of the secrets to David's success was his capacity to envision needs far beyond his own fading glory.

Abner: Man of Valor

Abner was a man with a long biblical history. We see him before the rise of David, working and fighting alongside Saul.

A man of considerable influence, he stood out as a towering lion-like figure. In fact during the time that Saul sought David's life, we find Abner leading the armies of Israel in search of David. On one specific occasion Abner, whose duty it was to guard the King, fell asleep while David and Abishai came into the camp and took a water cruse and spear. From the hillside the next day David spoke this concerning Abner, *"So David said to Abner, "Are you not a man? And who is like you in Israel? ..." (1 Samuel 26:15).*

Clearly this is a man of recognized stature in the nation. After the demise of Saul and Jonathan, Abner continued to follow the house of Saul by helping Ishbosheth, son of Saul, obtain the throne of Israel. This is the season wherein David ruled over the nation of Judah. For seven and a half years Abner stood as the Captain of the Host of Israel and against David, while Joab occupied a similar post for the tribe of Judah.

It is important for us to see the influence of Abner during this time. When Saul died it was Abner who was responsible for dividing the nation. It was Abner alone and his influence on Ishbosheth that persuaded him to align most of the tribes of Israel away from David. Had it not been for Abner, David would have ruled over a united Israel 7 years before the time he actually did. Then again, it was Abner who turned the other tribes to David and helped establish the Kingdom from Dan to Beersheba. Abner, in a moment of anger, makes the following declaration to Ishbosheth,

"Then Abner became very angry at the words of Ishbosheth, and said, "Am I a dog's head that belongs to Judah? Today I

*show loyalty to the house of Saul your father, to his brothers,
and to his friends, and have not delivered you into the hand of
David; and you charge me today with a fault concerning this
woman? [9] May God do so to Abner, and more also, if I do not
do for David as the LORD has sworn to him— [10] to transfer the
kingdom from the house of Saul, and set up the throne of
David over Israel and over Judah, from Dan to Beersheba" (2
Sam 3:8-10).*

This moment set up the transition for the whole nation to
come under David. The way David responds and treats Abner
after this is significant. Remember, David and Abner were
enemies , in effect for well over 7 long years. Consider how
many lives were lost on account of Abner. Imagine the kind
of disdain David might have developed during this period,
knowing that Abner was keeping him from his position as
rightful ruler of Israel. After all, it was David who was
anointed king over Israel and not Ishbosheth.

Even though Abner led the army of Saul and drove David to
the wilderness, there was no malice on David's part. A lesser
man would have harbored some sort of ill-will toward Abner
but David did not. Abner was chiefly responsible for delaying
the fulfillment of a prophetic word which declared David's
rightful ownership of the throne of Israel; despite that, David
demonstrates no vindictiveness. It is truly admirable that
David maintains a pure heart toward Abner, but this only tells
half the story.

Treachery and Reconciliation

Before the merging of Israel and Judah under David, there was a sequence of events wherein the brother of Joab, Asahel, was killed by Abner in battle. Asahel is pursuing Abner in the hopes of a great conquest. While running, Abner is pleading with Joab's brother to turn back. *"However, he refused to turn aside. Therefore Abner struck him in the stomach with the blunt end of the spear, so that the spear came out of his back; and he fell down there and died on the spot. So it was that as many as came to the place where Asahel fell down and died, stood still "(2 Samuel 2:23).* It was clear from the tale that Abner did his utmost to preserve the life of Asahel. Read Abner's plea!

"So Abner said again to Asahel, "Turn aside from following me. Why should I strike you to the ground? How then could I face your brother Joab?" (2 Samuel 2:22)

What he did was not out of pride, malice or revenge. The same could not be said of Asahel's brother Joab. Joab held vengeance in his heart and for years he was actually following a course of revenge. The moment he had the chance, after a treaty had been forged between Abner and David, Joab slew Abner with treachery. *"Now when Abner had returned to Hebron, Joab took him aside in the gate to speak with him privately, and there stabbed him in the stomach, so that he died for the blood of Asahel his brother"* *(2 Samuel 3:27).* Under the pretext of friendship, Joab's hatred and the culmination of seven years of bitterness unfolded.

This could have been David's posture, consumed with bitterness like Joab, but it was not. Instead, David's response to the death of Abner tells us a great deal about this incredible leader.

"And the king sang a lament over Abner and said: "Should Abner die as a fool dies?
Your hands were not bound Nor your feet put into fetters; As a man falls before wicked men, so you fell."

Then all the people wept over him again. And when all the people came to persuade David to eat food while it was still day, David took an oath, saying, "God do so to me, and more also, if I taste bread or anything else till the sun goes down!" 36 Now all the people took note of it, and it pleased them, since whatever the king did pleased all the people. 37 For all the people and all Israel understood that day that it had not been the king's intent to kill Abner the son of Ner. 38 Then the king said to his servants, "Do you not know that a prince and a great man has fallen this day in Israel? 39 And I am weak today, though anointed king; and these men, the sons of Zeruiah, are too harsh for me. The LORD shall repay the evildoer according to his wickedness." (2 Samuel 3:33-39)

David's deep sense of loss was clearly evident but it seems as though the significance of his heart posture is lost on us. Try to put yourself in his shoes by imagining some similar circumstance in your own life. Here David has waited for years to come into his destiny. He is forced to live in the desert, fleeing from one cave to another and even having to serve under the rule of heathen kings in a foreign land. Saul, who should have been a father to him, gives his wife to another and seeks to kill him. Finally, Saul dies and the open door to destiny stands clear. But just as David was about to enter Abner steps in and takes more than 90 percent away.

This kind of treachery can go very deep, yet, when reconciliation finally occurs David appears to forgive Abner. Still, it is one thing for David to permit Abner to serve him, it is quite another to return to normal relations. How could David not hold something back? How can one continue to walk as though nothing ever happened? This is the power of true reconciliation. David's words should ring deeply in us and speak of the power of total forgiveness.

And I am weak today, though anointed king; and these men, the sons of Zeruiah, are too harsh for me. The LORD shall repay the evildoer according to his wickedness." (2 Samuel 3:39)

The words reveal a man who has truly subjected his human nature to the mind and heart of God. David's capacity to honor is actually quite stunning. Most of us would have secretly rejoiced. We may not have said anything out loud but we all know what it is to harbor resentment. Then when tragedy befalls them it is their just due. It is as though we are vindicated and to us it is the evidence that God was on our side all along. On the other hand to speak with such depth and sincerity demonstrates David's ability to overlook his personal loss. It is clear personal ambition had been extinguished from David, and the glory of Israel was the only thing that mattered.

Kingdom Vision & Humility

We can see David's capacity for selflessness and forgiveness, but it actually goes further. David had a deep appreciation for those who served under him. He had the humility to understand it was not just himself, his skills and abilities as a king, which made him great, but the strength of those within his camp. While David could have been rejoicing that his ambitions had finally been realized, instead he mourned over the death of one former enemy. The depths of his mourning demonstrated a man with a clear vision and understanding of the components necessary to make the nation of Israel great.

David honored those who served him, not as a means of maintaining supremacy, but because he knew the truth that no leader is greater than those who serve in the realm of his influence. Now some might believe the tearing of his heart was a shrewd and calculated political move to curry favor. Those who would think such things testify to their own nature. In the case of David nothing could be further from the truth! David was a man with divine wisdom who knew from where his strength came. He understood the throne of

Israel was only as strong as those who served under its banner.

Today, when we survey the political landscape of the church, we see there is no lack of individuals boasting great vision. A few years ago there was a plethora of books praising the power of a vision. Suddenly everyone was talking about building schools and universities. Grandiose planning and projections were a given or you were not considered a 'real' leader. This may have looked like visionary leadership to some but mostly it was compensating for some other sense of weakness.

This approach is quite common when people have no actual plan or vision. Like Saul, whose actual vision constituted of him 'continuing as leader', many have not thought past their election or promotion. David demonstrated something far more than the railings of the ambitious. He possessed the God-given evidence of an understanding which must undergird a genuine vision.

Building something of enduring quality takes more than vision, it takes understanding. Every architect will tell you that the foundation of a building determines its height. The extension arm of a crane is not solely dependent upon its own composition and physical structure but on the counter-balance within the base. In like manner the outreach potential of a church is limited by the strength of ministries which add to its core. David understood this!

Leadership in the Church

The reason the Lord gave the five-fold ministry for the equipping of the saints was that it would take five different kinds of leaders and ministries. He made them to be interdependent so that the cumulative effect of their ministries would produce a mature expression of Christ. The leader who cannot appreciate the need for each of these ministries to function at the core of a Church will handicap himself and his vision. This short-sighted person will want everyone to think and act like himself.

Those who do not understand this principle of leadership risks destroying the very thing they are trying to create. Countless times we have heard and seen insecure leaders alienate strong personalities and ministries within their congregations for fear of losing control or being usurped. What a tragedy! It is the strength and value of these same personalities and ministries which bolster the effectiveness of the leader. To some the mantra is 'get rid of the strong ones- they will only rise up to challenge your place'. In fact one can actually measure the strength of a leader based on how many other strong personalities are willing to work with him.

David understood this. When Abner made Ishbosheth the son of Saul king over all Israel, it became Joab's license to continue the feud. In the mind of David the feud only went one way. David wanted and needed Abner! His heart and posture clearly said, 'Abner you may think I am your enemy, but I will not make you mine'! He refused to allow anyone to determine who his enemy was. Again his words should linger in our ears. *"And I am weak today, though anointed king..." (2 Samuel 3:39).*

Taking Stock

The malicious and spiteful leader is no leader at all—he is a child. The one who is unmoved or relieved over the departure of the strong is one who will not extend far past his borders. This is not to say that we tolerate sedition; rather we cannot be intimidated by the gifted and the strong. There is a breadth of perspective a leader must have and it can only come from the Lord. To be like David we must have a heart which can embrace a large circle of people. If we cannot mourn at the loss of those who appear to be against us, then we are perhaps more like Saul than David. If we actively pursue the expulsion and destruction of those who threaten our leadership, make no mistake about it, we are exactly like Saul.

6   CONFLICT

'Strength and good leadership are not a series of behaviors but a manifestation of a life deeply rooted in the One who is strong.'

Dealing with Conflict

Managing conflict is a critical skill for any leader. Perhaps this is one of the reasons the Lord gives us children; they give us ample opportunity to sharpen our skills. Initially, we can use the fact that we are older, smarter and stronger as our key mediation tools. Eventually these rivers run dry and children begin to find fault with us as parents. As the years go by they begin to match us in the areas of intelligence and strength. This is where true leadership can emerge as victor. When there are no more trump cards like, 'go to bed' and the ever popular 'because I said so', we must find a better arsenal at our disposal. Examining our methods and experiences in the light of some Biblical examples of conflict can both gauge our performance and illustrate qualities of great leaders.

A Vital Key

David excelled in the area of conflict management. He possessed a rare ability to solve problems and win the respect of those around him. As King it would have been easy to rely on his title or God-given right to 'be in charge'. However, titles, while not wrong, can only go so far. It is right to teach people to honor authority, as they are well served by adopting this posture, but leaders should not count on it. Those who hide behind their titles will not successfully lead anyone. When there is not a stable and inspirational leadership behind the title, chaos will eventually follow.

David did not rule by force, by accident or by appointed authority. His authority was rooted in the fact that he became and was born a gifted leader. The truth is that we cannot all be natural leaders, but we can learn from the experience and example of other great leaders. Learning to resolve conflict is a key area. If we have any hope of serving as leaders, then this is a pivotal point in our quest. In David's interactions with the very influential Joab, he demonstrates a critical aspect of leadership, which may be one of the key reasons behind the longevity of his rule. Before we can look at how David handled this challenge, let's look at how Ishbosheth dealt with a similar problem.

After the demise of Saul and Jonathan the empire falls into two camps. The tribe of Judah followed David while the rest of Israel congregated behind Ishbosheth, the son of Saul. Serving at the helm of Israel's army was Abner who was instrumental in preserving the house of Saul. In what seems to be the first recorded challenge to Ishbosheth's leadership we find Abner sleeping with one of Saul's concubines. This was an attempt to identify with the throne. To his credit Ishbosheth was quick to recognize the challenge and spoke up.

"And Saul had a concubine, whose name was Rizpah, the daughter of Aiah. So Ishbosheth said to Abner, "Why have you gone in to my father's concubine?" (2 Samuel 3:7)

The rebuke was clearly not well received. The scene finds Abner raving with rage at Ishbosheth.

"Then Abner became very angry at the words of Ishbosheth, and said, "Am I a dog's head that belongs to Judah? Today I show loyalty to the house of Saul your father, to his brothers, and to his friends, and have not delivered you into the hand of David; and you charge me today with a fault concerning this woman? (2 Samuel 3:8)

This was a defining moment. While it brings up many issues it really touches on the question of Ishbosheth's right to rule. Abner is taking credit for the throne of Saul and is quite willing to receive payment. He feels he is owed something from Ishbosheth. In situations like these when one's leadership is being questioned, the response is always a manifestation of either faith or fear. It exposes the heart of our motivations.

Ishbosheth is now faced with the reality of his quest to be

king and if he believes God is in it or not. A man of faith lives out of what God provides whereas a natural man seizes opportunities. True conviction is a place of supernatural strength, and the issue now revolves around the depth of Ishbosheth's conviction.

One could argue that his personality was too weak for a man like Abner. But personalities have no effect when our sustaining strength is derived from the stated will of God. The real question is not about strength of personality but about conviction. Conviction answers the question, 'why do you have the right to rule'. A man of faith knows that promotion comes from above and not from the arm of flesh. Had Ishbosheth been convinced of this he could have stood his ground. Instead, he does not rise to the occasion and scurries off to some insignificant corner. The fallout is described as follows: *"And he could not answer Abner another word, because he feared him." (2 Samuel 3:11)*

The most telling element of this encounter is the fear. When we are opportunistic we can only be hopeful. A hopeful leader is a weak leader. A true leader has strength rooted in conviction and a sense of destiny. His strength is not from egotism or the sense of entitlement so often parading as conviction, but a calling that has emerged from at the very least a sense of providence. Ishbosheth did not have the benefit of actual conviction and was therefore easily usurped. Abner's ability to intimidate is not a question of his own motivation; it is a result of Ishbosheth's lack of confidence. Clearly, Ishbosheth knew that the only reason he had a hope of being king was because of Abner.

The intimidation factor probably grew as a matter of course as Abner served sacrificially for the cause of the house of Saul. There is a developing dynamic within these situations, which every leader must be aware of in order to maintain his position as the leader. The tendency in the minds and hearts of those who sacrifice for the 'cause' is that they deserve special status. They begin to feel responsible for the success of the leader and should therefore be exempt from proper behavior. Abner fell into this mindset and Ishbosheth was too unsure of himself and insecure concerning his role to resist a sense of indebtedness to Abner.

A Similar Situation

A few years ago I ran into a similar situation. It was not someone rising up against me but a question of whether I was called to lead in a certain organization. When I was offered the position, I declined thinking it was not what God had for me. After a few more requests it became clear that God wanted me to reconsider. I waited for months until the Lord revealed to me in a powerful visitation the call to accept the position & move. Once I accepted the position, the political fight began within the organization.

I was, however, free from the realm of that political spirit. God had spoken to me, and my right to be the leader in this situation was not based on my skills or lack thereof but upon divine providence. It was not important for others to see this, but it was critical for me to know this. When Ishbosheth was challenged he did not have the benefit of this conviction.

The second factor speaks to the inroads a political spirit tries to make in the life of a leader. When the egos of leaders are fed by their love of title and position they are susceptible and cannot help but begin to make grave errors. Once given over to this kind of selfish ambition the downward spiral begins. Jesus declared that the prince of this world was coming but that he had nothing in Jesus *"I will no longer talk much with you, for the ruler of this world is coming, and he has nothing in Me." (John 14:30).* In other words, there was no covetousness or any desire Satan could promise that would interest Him. The point being when we have ego needs that agree with Satan, he can find something to latch onto.

For me, as it pertained to this position, I neither sought nor wanted the position. In fact, in my mind it seemed a step down from where I was functioning and I did not fully understand why God would even want me there. I did not need or desire the position to fulfill a personal ambition so could not be intimidated by the political spirit. Already convinced of what God had given, I knew that what God had given no one could take away. On the other hand, had I tried to obtain that position through charm, appropriate gifting or modified behavior, I would have been in trouble. Leaders who do not function from a place of providence cannot maintain peace during conflict. They fear losing what they have.

Power Struggle

Abner was already *'strengthening his hold on the house of Saul' (2 Samuel 3:6)*. Abner was capable and strong in both his physical prowess and person. Ishbosheth's feeble attempt at damage control was obviously far too late, and was bolstered by very little <u>'commanding respect'</u>. We can only speculate, but it seems quite probable that in other situations, Ishbosheth had also demonstrated enough shortcomings to lose any possibility of ongoing control.

Within the ranks of any kingdom or people group over which one may be given the responsibility to lead, there will and must be individuals who try our leadership abilities. The most difficult people to lead are the strongest and sometimes the most suited for leadership themselves. Our capacity to lead lies in our ability to govern the strong with grace, wisdom and mercy. Leadership, in this sense is not unlike the bridling and breaking of a stallion.

Many leaders lose respect of followers when they over respond to challenges. Innocent probing can sometimes illicit dramatic retorts from insecure leaders. These dramatic responses include a kind of fear and panic. These are often associated with attempts to maintain your hold and is in fact, weakness. What is in the heart of a leader will emerge in times of trial and conflict and will become a barometer of that leader's capacity. It is important to note this does not justify sedition of any kind; rather, it is meant to be a plum line for those who lead.

We must be sure to underscore that strong does not mean rebellious, lest we give license to the self-willed. In the context of the Church, the strong are those with divine calling and anointing, whose dedication and understanding of the Kingdom of God challenges our own. If we can successfully obtain and maintain the loyalty and respect of these, the sphere of our leadership will continue to grow. David was able to do this.

It is clear that Ishbosheth was unable to govern and lead Abner, yet when David was faced with similar challenges, he prevailed. Joab and the other sons of Zeruiah were formidable men in their own right. At one point David was even found lamenting at the difficulty of the sons of Zeruiah. Despite this, he was able to retain their respect and harness their abilities to ensure a prosperous reign. The key difference between Ishbosheth and David, although evident in many ways, is most clearly obvious through David's lack of insecurity and fear. Ishbosheth feared the influence of Abner whereas David rested in unwavering confidence unmoved, though sometimes perplexed by these sons of Zeruiah.

Joab's Strength

David's perception of his own ability to lead Joab was never influenced by Joab's dominant position in the national affairs of Israel. The success of Joab could not intimidate David since David was not insecure. This confidence was evident in David's ability to take Joab's advice during his deep mourning over Absalom (2 Samuel 18:29-33). In this scenario Joab rebukes David for loathing the sacrifice of the nation by mourning Absalom's death. Instead of celebrating the preservation of the monarchy the people experience shame. Listen to the stern manner of Joab's rebuke:

"Then Joab came into the house to the king, and said, "Today you have disgraced all your servants who today have saved your life, the lives of your sons and daughters, the lives of your wives and the lives of your concubines, in that you love your enemies and hate your friends. For you have declared today that you regard neither princes nor servants; for today I perceive that if Absalom had lived and all of us had died today, then it would have pleased you well. Now therefore, arise, go out and speak comfort to your servants. For I swear by the LORD, if you do not go out, not one will stay with you this night. And that will be worse for you than all the evil that has befallen you from your youth until now." (2 Samuel 19:5-7).

What was David's response? He arose and sat in the gate! An insecure leader would not have recognized the wisdom of Joab's words. A lesser man would have been deeply offended, even outraged over the disrespectful tone of Joab's stern monologue. A characteristic of a strong leader is that he is able to hear wisdom from any source. A weak leader will instead display an air of control and superiority and overextend himself with efforts to defend authority which has not even been challenged.

This poses a difficulty for those who would want to be strong leaders and are not. Some may even be reading this to discover the right way to posture oneself. This is not what this revelation is intended to produce. Rather, the truth is a measuring rod. It reveals what is actually within us, not so that we can change a posture but to produce repentance to be followed by humility and ultimately faith. Insecurity, when brought to the light, should trigger in us a deep cry to the Lord for grace. David's life was an example of good leadership which emerged from a revelation of God. Strength and good leadership are not a series of behaviors but a manifestation of a life deeply rooted in the One who is strong.

The Evidence

The extent of David's security was also evident in the way he dealt with Joab's ungodly acts. After Abner was slain in treachery by Joab, David did not flinch for a second to consider the great sacrifice and contributions made by Joab. This is in stark contrast to Ishbosheth who fell prey to that common human weakness – a sense of indebtedness to men. David had a healthy regard for the contributions of Joab, but it did not compromise his view of righteousness. He immediately and publicly denounced Joab's ungodly actions. Furthermore, he raised a lament at the grave and leads the people in national mourning: *"And the king sang a lament over Abner and said: "Should Abner die as a fool dies? Your hands were not bound nor your feet put into fetters; As a man falls before wicked men, so you fell." Then all the people wept over him again (2 Samuel 3:33-34).*

David seemed to intuitively know the right response. He didn't waste time considering whether the outcome of his decision would be popular or not. There were no political balloons being 'floated' nor was there an 'Angus Reid' survey to gauge public response. He functioned out of principle and truth. The deed was wicked and David did not fail to say as much. There was no inclination to alter his response or even consider the implications for Joab. No weight was given to how disenfranchised Joab might feel. David's commitment was squarely toward the righteous God and he was unwilling to compromise, even if political-correctness might extend the length of his rule.

The very presence of strong forceful people, like Joab or Abner, would frustrate a weaker man into crisis. Most men, like Ishbosheth, would have retreated rather than face the possibility of conflict. David understood that strong men are undamaged by strong responses. He also knew that strength is not the same as rebellion. This is critical and is in itself a monumental truth. Weak leaders often confuse strength for rebellion and therefore reward passivity. This posture is one of the most destructive forces in any administration. But they honestly believe loyalty means agreement – when they speak, you nod. The truth is that the higher a leader goes the more he requires and values the opinions and advice of others. David was just such a man.

Which of you...

The presence of strong people legitimizes the position we take. Consider the ministry of Jesus. While He may have had an authoritarian veneer it was only because He was right. This was not blind stubbornness masquerading as confidence. He left a lot of room for appeals and was not adverse to discussion. In fact He encouraged the sharing of ideas as revealed through His interactions with the religious leaders. Knowing their hearts, He understood they were of another mind. While they lacked the courage to face him directly, Jesus invites open challenge. *"Which of you convicts Me of sin? And if I tell the truth, why do you not believe Me?" (John 8:46).* He was saying *'let us reason together'*; you bring your wisdom and I will bring mine. Those who are more concerned with being right and appearing strong would never consider such a proposition. They would only enter the proverbial 'ring' if circumstances were stacked in their favor. Why? Because neither wisdom nor righteousness are part of their aim – to them it is all about position and control!

For principled leaders, the goal of staying in office is not central. David was the kind of leader that was more interested in the truth. Therefore he was not shy about challenging others, neither was he hesitant to be challenged.

Challenges to our leadership, such as the ones faced by David and Ishbosheth, are not a curse but a blessing. They are designed to reveal the flaws and strengths in our efforts to lead. They offer us the opportunity to solidify or modify our stance. Those who are insecure cannot afford to honestly evaluate where they stand or why. Their insecurity makes them defensive to the point where the only priority is to appear strong.

Strong people are from the Lord; they help us to become better–or at the very least, more honest leaders. The opportunities for improvement and growth usually materialize on the field of conflict. If we run from conflict we demonstrate one of two things—either an unwillingness to evaluate our present condition or a fear of man and a general lack of internal strength. Either of these will limit our usefulness in the program of the Lord. It is in the best interest of all who feel the call to leadership to anticipate and value these kinds of challenges. Conflict does not have to be seen as a challenge to our leadership, but the proof of it.

7   DAVID STYLE LEADERSHIP

David was said to have a heart after God. Many of us talk
about His courage and the victories on the battle field, but his
most heroic trait was his faith. This was evident throughout
his private and public life. The most profound elements of his
faith are found in the way he handled the hardships. Some
might argue that he brought trouble on himself (which he
sometimes did). Nevertheless, this never stopped lesser men
from rebelling and running from the authority of God. The
scriptures are replete with examples of the kings of Judah and
Israel who not only rejected the Word of the Lord, but
persecuted and killed His prophets. During the most difficult
times and throughout stern discipline of the Lord, David
remained faithful. Not only did he not reject the Word of the
Lord, but more than that, he received the Word in a way that
reveals a deep understanding of the heart of God. He seemed
to have knowledge of something the Apostle Paul would write
about many years later *"Therefore consider the goodness and
severity of God: ..." (Rom 11:22).*

Yielding to God

As one might imagine the Kingdom of God will require God at the center. Since *"..."Every kingdom divided against itself is brought to desolation, and every city or house divided against itself will not stand" (Matthew 12:25).* His supremacy will not be challenged or ignored. The recruitment criteria for leaders places a high premium on the ability to yield to Him and the test of allegiance is therefore central to our training. Leadership in the Kingdom of God demands that we love and honor the Lord and His Word, both the goodness and the severity. It is not hard to embrace the goodness of God but yielding to His severity requires true faith. Faith believes in the wisdom and righteousness of God; that God is actually greater than us in every conceivable way.

Growing up in a military family and spending a few years in Cadets, I have a decent insight into the 'chain of command'. This has helped cement an understanding of obedience since military training emphasizes explicit obedience. The reason is simple and could save your life. When you are on the battlefield and the commander yells 'Duck!', you do not want to be the one musing over the command. Life and death hang in the balance. Civilians can afford to question and wonder because the atmosphere they find themselves in is very different. The advancement of God's Kingdom is more military than civilian emphasizing the need to learn explicit obedience. In the end it might just define our placement in God's overall plan.

Parenting can likewise expose aspects of the Kingdom. Every parent has faced the predicament where a child is reluctant and we cannot take the time to explain. Worse yet, is when the explanation is beyond them. At those precise moments we might use the words 'trust me'. Indeed, when we stand in eternity looking upon the history of our journey we might see the very same thing: That is, God high above us in our moments of struggle simply asking that we trust Him.

Heavenly Judgment

As already mentioned, our natural disposition is to respond to the goodness of God. We, who are by nature lovers of convenience and ease, are disposed toward His goodness. This has meant we always look for the easy and pleasant promises. We

> *It is never the Lord's will to bring evil, however, hardship, discipline and pruning are necessary to bring one into their destiny.*

search out the scriptures to discover what exquisite privileges and rights we have as His children. Which is fine! It is necessary to discover God's heart for us. However, it becomes problematic when it disposes us to avoiding discipline. Often we talk of loving the whole counsel of God but we do a pretty good job of avoiding every hint of unpleasantness. How often have we confessed and claimed the promise of discipline belonging to those who are sons? It is part of our inheritance so we should contend for it as it is the preeminent evidence of our sonship. *"And you have forgotten the exhortation which speaks to you as to sons:*

" My son, do not despise the chastening of the LORD, nor be discouraged when you are rebuked by Him; For whom the LORD loves He chastens, And scourges every son whom He receives." If you endure chastening, God deals with you as with sons; for what son is there whom a father does not chasten? But if you are without chastening, of which all have become partakers, then you are illegitimate and not sons. Furthermore, we have had human fathers who corrected us, and we paid them respect. Shall we not much more readily be in subjection to the Father of spirits and live? For they indeed for a few days chastened us as seemed best to them, but He for our profit, that we may be partakers of His holiness. Now no chastening seems to be joyful for the present, but painful; nevertheless, afterward it yields the peaceable fruit of righteousness to those who have been trained by it" (Hebrews 12:5-11).

These types of passages are found in abundance. The 'exaggerated' point being, if left to ourselves we would, like children, choose dessert over broccoli (all due respect to broccoli). The long-term result would be physical impoverishment. Likewise, in the walk of a believer, the perspective of the mature instinctively knows a continuous diet of pleasant things is fundamentally unhealthy. It leads to spiritual impoverishment. The responsible leader, who truly loves the Lord and His Word, will not refuse Him, even when He is being harsh.

David demonstrated himself to be a man who truly loved the Lord and did not reject His counsel. His devotion to the Lord did not hinge on the promise of comfort or greatness. It is never the Lord's will to bring evil, however, hardship, discipline and pruning are necessary to bring one into their destiny. Faith enables us to embrace the training only God knows we need. Deep in David's consciousness was a conviction that God could be trusted above all else. This sentiment is reflected in the following moment when judgment was required on the nation. The prophet gives David several different options but David throws himself toward the Lord. *"... David said to Gad, "I am in great distress. Please let us fall into the hand of the LORD, for His mercies are great; but do not let me fall into the hand of man"* (2 Sam 24:14).

Whatever may come, David knew the very best option was to do what was necessary to draw closer to the Lord. This conviction, reflected in many of the Psalms, enabled David to receive all that God's Word declared. Even when the Word of the Lord was unpleasant David trembled and feared the Lord. This was especially obvious in Absalom's rebellion. When Absalom rebelled and plotted against him, David waited for the process to run its course. God had already spoken through the prophet what would happen. *"Now therefore, the sword shall never depart from your house, because you have despised Me, and have taken the wife of Uriah the Hittite to be your wife.' Thus says the LORD: 'Behold, I will raise up adversity against you from your own house; and I will take*

your wives before your eyes and give them to your neighbor,
and he shall lie with your wives in the sight of this sun" (2
Samuel 12:10-11).

This Word came as a result of David's sin. Unfortunately, it
was the son he loved who would be a central figure in the
Word. This is not to say that anything Absalom did was born
of God. His motivation was evil inside and out. Accepting the
Word of God for our lives does not mean we must accept the
evil intent as done by others. We must simply look past them
believing God to be greater than their intentions. In the life of
Joseph when his brothers sold him into slavery, Joseph
plainly stated, "*'But as for you, you meant evil against me; but*
God meant it for good, in order to bring it about as it is this
day, to save many people alive" (Genesis 50:20). From God's
perspective the betrayal by the brothers is still tallied as sin.
The fact that God, in His fantastic wisdom, can use the
disobedience of man speaks well of Him and not those who
perpetrate evil. This duality confuses men since we like to
categorize things as either good or evil. Situations like these
cross the lines. If we are going to have a proper
understanding we need to be able to see these scenarios
through a larger grid than merely right and wrong or good
and evil.

In this case David was forced to leave his post in Jerusalem
and appeared to lose some part of his inheritance. He did
not sulk or throw old promises into the face of God, nor did
He blame it on Satan. Rather, through faith he humbled
himself and appealed to the mercy of God, all the while being

careful to acknowledge the authority of the Lord in his life. This was something of the severity of God, and while unpleasant, it was still the outcome of the Word of the Lord. Unlike many others, David had the kind of humility and discernment needed to honor the Lord and take what was coming to him.

Shimei

Later as David and his men traveled to safety they were confronted by a man called Shimei; a member of the household of Saul. In response to this man's cursing and rock throwing, one of David's men requested permission to dismember him. Listen to David's response!

"But the king said, "What have I to do with you, you sons of Zeruiah? So let him curse, because the LORD has said to him, 'Curse David.' Who then shall say, 'Why have you done so?'" And David said to Abishai and all his servants, "See how my son who came from my own body seeks my life. How much more now may this Benjamite? Let him alone, and let him curse; for so the LORD has ordered him." (2 Samuel 16:10-11)

Here is another example of David's teachable heart. He takes humiliation which is neither deserved nor appropriate. His stance differs from what we often see in people when they are being disciplined. Usually there is a feverish attempt to escape culpability. Not with David! He could have shouted out to the Lord saying, *'All right already, I heard you and I said I was sorry. Why do you have to keep rubbing it into my face?'*

He could have had Shimei immediately killed which, as king, was easily justified. After all, this matter was between himself and God. Who was Shimei to think he should berate David? The fact is David knew Shimei had no right, but he humbly chose to take the low road, and through this he was appealing to the mercy of God in faith. He knew God loved Him and the Lord's hand would overturn events sooner rather than later.

Some might interpret this situation altogether differently. Our usual human approach is to question whether Shimei was right or wrong but David understood the question to be a side issue. The real exercise is contrite humility before God. David could and would deal with the man later. The moment required receiving discipline with humility to turn the heart of God. David appealed to the mercy of God by submission rather than responding in wrath toward others – Shimei included. Our typical approach is to deflect and escape. This is the approach my children have taken when I try to discipline them. Rather than fully embracing the consequence of their action they try to bring my attention to others. While what the other child did or is doing may not be correct, I am more disturbed by their lack of contriteness. In that moment I want to see humility and godly sorrow. Children instead focus on attempting to lessen their culpability by raising the guilt of others. This is counterproductive! David understood this and so focused on humility rather than whether or not Shimei was crossing a line.

This whole concept can be quite tricky and difficult to understand, especially if we are of the mind that God is only responsible for the pleasant things which come our way. You may even ask yourself, *'Why would God be orchestrating such terrible seditions in the land?'* Or in response you may say, *'let us not be naive, this is the work of Satan and not God'*. Yet, scripture is clear: there is a human element that opens the door to judgment. Even so, these decrees given by the prophet to David were specifically released by the authority of the Word of the Lord. There are times when the Lord covers a sin then releases us without dire consequence, but this was not one of them. For whatever reason this sin had to have public consequence. David's affair with Bathsheba and the murder of her husband must be dealt with. Thus, the secret sin was to be brought before the whole nation.

"For you did it secretly, but I will do this thing before all Israel, before the sun." (2 Samuel 12:12)

One significant aspect of this discipline is the Lord's implication of Himself. He was not shy about identifying himself the party responsible for this judgment, nor is it likely He was as misinformed or purposefully ambiguous. If God is not afraid to speak in these terms neither should we be timid. This declaration was from the mouth of God and was therefore the Word of God. David accepted the full weight of this judgment. When it came to dealing with Shimei, David did not resist the hand of God but chose instead to honor the

Lord by submitting. A man who truly honors the Lord will love his discipline as well as his blessings.

A man of understanding has the foresight to know the discipline of the Lord is a blessing. The Word of the Lord is always good because God is not capable of evil. God's severity is not evil! Every Word is a treasure given to reveal the heart of God and imparts His nature. The discipline of the Lord releases something of the character of our Father and increases our capacity for His presence. David had an honest love of the truth. He could not bring himself to despise the Word of the Lord, even if that same Word meant suffering under difficult circumstances. His integrity would not allow him to become double-minded concerning God and His Word. If God's Word brought life to David's bones, then all of His Words were to be received with gladness.

Honoring the Word

Now honoring God did not require David to become the scourge of the earth, so to speak, and enduring the whims of individuals like Shimei. But, as I already wrote, David knew the tender mercies of God and that the Lord would show Himself to be kind to the humble. David knew the Lord; he had a sense of what would move the heart of God towards mercy. As a father myself I know I respond much better to the child that is contrite when I am disciplining. The obstinate one automatically gets a stronger response from me. Any attempt by a child to correct my correction is met with further discipline and not mercy. So there is a time for bowing low and a time for making a case. David knew the difference. Do we?

In the case of Bathsheba's child David knew to pray and fast, whereas in this case with Shimei, he knew it was best to silently endure. Herein are two seemingly similar situations with two radically different approaches. This is because a son who truly knows his father knows when to speak and when to remain silent. In the matter of Bathsheba's son David did not succeed in saving the life of the child. Whereas in the case of Shimei, David's musings were correct when he said:

"It may be that the LORD will look on my affliction, and that the LORD will repay me with good for his cursing this day." (2 Samuel 16:12)

David's faith and knowledge of God are evident in this situation in that he defers all things to the hand of God. This is not to be confused with a kind of theological fatalism. When people are ignorant of the heart of God, they fall to legal interpretations. This results in a resistance of circumstance or rejection of hardship. True faith and relationship is not so rigid. Rather, using the benefit of his relationship with the Lord, he skillfully and wisely navigates between God's willing bent toward mercy and His need to execute justice. David is an example of one who fully honors the Word of the Lord without being a passive victim of circumstances. He had the honesty and integrity of heart to recognize the hand of God and did not waste time justifying himself. He interacted with the reality of the situation by benefiting from discipline without prolonging it. This was a remarkable testimony to the depth of his insight into God.

Interpreting Discipline

Learning from David is critical especially given the current and past trends of the Body of Christ. It has become popular to interpret the work of God and the devil on the basis of principles. We have simplistically begun to differentiate what is God and what is the enemy by the level of happiness a situation creates for us. This is a mistake as it creates a presupposition that can skew our interpretation of scripture such as the following: *"The thief does not come except to steal, and to kill, and to destroy. I have come that they may have life, and that they may have it more abundantly" (John 10:10).*

Jesus tells us in this verse He is for us and not against us. Unfortunately many have taken this to mean much more. The passage in essence underlines the motive of Satan and the motive of God, but it tells nothing about the ways and means of either. Some would suggest this passage informs us that everything unpleasant is automatically from Satan and must be steadfastly resisted.

Think in terms of a parent saying this to their child, *'My son I have come not to steal, kill or destroy but that you might have an abundant life.'* A parent might need to clarify this position after imposing discipline. If this is our only reference then discipline might have the appearance of cruelty. When children are grounded from television, sent to their room or made to do homework and chores they do not enjoy, we assure them this is for their good. The discipline and hardship will shape the character of a child but in the eyes of the 12 year old it is not abundant life, but this is where it leads.

It is in vain that a child would remind a father with the words, *'You're supposed to be for me and not against me.',* or *'You said I was supposed to be the head and not the tail.'* In this context it is very clear that the pain the father is going to inflict is for the benefit of the child. If we could hear the Father He would be saying "'Yes!' 'Because I **want** you to be the head and not the tail I am training you for righteousness.'" The promise is not about circumstance so much as it is about destination. The fact that God has promised to be for us or that he wishes us to succeed, is not criteria for determining what it will take to get there. If we are going to encourage people to honor the Lord and His Word, we must encourage them to honor a word or circumstances of discipline as well.

Paul's letter to the Corinthian Church tells us that if we do not judge ourselves, that is, properly evaluate our responsibility in service to God, and then the Lord will judge us.

*"For this reason many are weak and sick among you, and
many sleep. For if we would judge ourselves, we would not be
judged. But when we are judged, we are chastened by the
Lord, that we may not be condemned with the world"* (1
Corinthians 11:30-32).

This passage follows Paul's rebuke to the Corinthians for their
reckless behavior toward one another. They were a Church
full of selfish power-hungry individuals who had no regard for
one another and could not see Christ in their brothers. The
Word of God to them at that time was rightfully one of
judgment and chastening, despite the fact the Lord's ultimate
and greatest intention was they go higher.

In the parable of the sower, the one who bears fruit from the
Word of God is the one who *"... having heard the word with a
noble and good heart, keep it and bear fruit with patience"
(Luke 8:15).* David demonstrated his complete commitment
to trust and serve the Lord, by receiving His discipline. If we
are to be Christians and leaders after a Biblical example, let us
then devote ourselves to loving the whole counsel of God. It
is fundamentally dishonest to be in a family for the purpose of
receiving the benefits, while at the same time refusing the
discipline of the Father of that household. If David has
demonstrated anything for us, it certainly must include an
honest heart. He stands as a shining example of a man whose
heart was truly for the Lord.

8   DAVID AND SAUL

There are many abilities which lend themselves to making one great in the eyes of God and people, but none so necessary as unwavering faith expressed through patience. Patience is key. The very nature of patience implies a time component. We inherit the promises of God through faith and patience (Hebrew 6:12). A conviction rarely found in this present day is; 'God is in control' in whatever circumstances we find ourselves. While it might appear to be too Calvinistic for some, it was a deep seated belief in the heart of David. It was not a passive belief that made him a victim, but a vibrant confidence in the power of God that released the hand of God to work on his behalf. To develop this kind of faith takes a peculiar journey. If we will be wise or great, we must learn to embrace the challenge of adversity, with a confession which states *all things work together for good'*. To some this is the empty retort of a fatalistic victim, while to those who understand its power it is the catalyst that causes things to work together for good. True faith releases the hand of God, while restraining the hand of man.

Adversity

David experienced firsthand the adversity of faith. That is, his situation gave him no option except waiting while He trusted God to come through. This is tremendously difficult for men to withstand as we much prefer a course requiring some kind of action. Inaction is a deep kind of death. David was compelled to believe in the Lord's ability to fulfill His promise without human strength.

After having been anointed as king of Israel, David was forced to wait patiently in very obscure surroundings for the fullness of the promise. Like Israel coming out of Egypt with the 'promised land' in view, he was forced to journey through a barren wilderness. Reaching a promise often means enduring the opposite until we reach the fullness of time. The real test of David's belief was seen when God placed opportunities before him to *self-fulfill* his destiny.

On two occasions we see David bypassing opportunities to destroy Saul, who was the only barrier between him and his destiny. Saul, rather than becoming a father to David, viewed him as competition and forced him to flee into the wilderness. It was there that David was given the opportunity to prematurely enter his destiny. The first time was in the cave of En Gedi where David and his men were hiding. Saul went into the cave to 'attend to his needs' and David cut off the corner of Saul's robe. When David confronted Saul, he declared his continued allegiance saying, *"As the proverb of the ancients says, 'Wickedness proceeds from the wicked.' But my hand shall not be against you" (1 Samuel 24:13).* Saul was convicted and turned back from pursuing David, only to rekindle his hatred of David a while later.

The strength of David's commitment was demonstrated in this moment. Not only did he not kill Saul, but when he addressed Saul, he did so on his knees with his face to the ground (1 Samuel 24:8). How rare is this kind of honor! Consider the tendency we have to disrespect those who are not perfect in our eyes. How often have we belittled, criticized and dishonored leaders for much less than what Saul had done. The integrity of David should stand as a brilliant example of what it means to honor the Lord and those who serve him. But to David it was more than an issue of honor – it had to do with faith. David did not war in the realm of the natural and so he was not willing to view Saul as the impedance to his own future. David could continue honoring imperfect leaders because he trusted God with his destiny. His faith kept him from taking his destiny into his own hands.

The second time was similar to the first as once again Saul hunted David in the wilderness. David and Abishai crept into Saul's camp where Abner, Saul's chief guardian and his men were sleeping. When Abishai requested Saul's death, David answered:

"But David said to Abishai, "Do not destroy him; for who can stretch out his hand against the LORD's anointed, and be

guiltless?" [10] *David said furthermore, "As the LORD lives, the LORD shall strike him, or his day shall come to die, or he shall go out to battle and perish" (1 Samuel 26:9-10).*

Again David chooses honor and restraint when he could have easily justified revenge. Blind ambition creates this kind of vengeance while it rationalizes murder. David would tolerate nothing of the sort. He had no sense of entitlement despite his promise, neither did not consider it a small matter that God had chosen Saul as king. Despite the clear fact that Saul was unfit to represent the Lord, David considered it a matter for the Lord to deal with. This is the ultimate posture of faith. It does not mean we do nothing, but it does mean we avoid even the smallest similitude of self-promotion. When we are the chief beneficiaries of a strategy we should always be leery of our motives. We guard our heart and protect our faith from corruption by not allowing ourselves to believe the lie that we act on God's behalf.

Jesus instructed His disciples to turn the other cheek (Luke 6:29). This is not a call to utter passivity but to a journey beyond oneself. The problem with man is his self-centered nature. There is something inside man that permitted, would subjugate the entire world to himself. Opportunity is often the only thing standing between Hitler and us. The principle Jesus was calling us to walk in takes the wrath of man out of the equation. It does not mean we cannot pursue justice, instead it asks that we make sure we are actually pursuing justice. To do that the human element must be removed.

The disciples of Jesus were quick to pursue their manner of justice, suggesting calling down fire: *"And when His disciples James and John saw this, they said, "Lord, do You want us to command fire to come down from heaven and consume them, just as Elijah did?" (Luke 9:54).* They had substituted their own need for honor for the heart of God. Jesus quickly judges their wickedness declaring *"...'You do not know what manner of spirit you are of" (Luke 9:55).* Like our own journey and David's before us, it involves a deep purging of our souls. The Spirit of God leads us down a path that continually requires denial of our basest instincts.

The disciples were being trained to reach into heaven to change the earth. Their default seemed to be 'reach into hell' – metaphorically speaking. We access one of two realms each and every time we try to change the earth. Faith touches heaven, whereas impatience, anger, and the like, reaches into hell. Even when we try to do good, it is far too easy to do evil. David's training meant walking in dire circumstances. He was forced to live contrary to his destiny while resisting every urge to bring the promise to pass in his own strength. It is the proverbial carrot before the donkey – a test to see if he will lunge out of season.

To his credit David believed in the sovereign rule of God. He did not believe God looks passively from a distance at the affairs of men, but that He interacts with the intimate details of each of our daily lives. David believed in the power of God to deliver. His struggle was maintaining that belief in the face of mounting evidence to the contrary. Having heard the prophetic declaration from Samuel, David believed his place was assured by the Lord Himself. Yet, the tension between this and the reality of his hermitic exile must have been excruciating. Herein is the testing of faith, where we have the option to either forsake the promise, take matters into our own hands, or maintain the course. David exercised his faith. His tried conviction is later recorded in the Psalms as he writes: *"For exaltation comes neither from the east nor from the west nor from the south. But God is the Judge: He puts down one, and exalts another"* (Ps. 75:6-7).

Two Sides of Faith

Despite the strength of David's patient faith, there were also times when another posture was required. When it came to Goliath, David took immediate and decisive action. He did not go aside to pray and fast, but instinctively rose to the occasion. Both expressions are valid as long as they are catalyzed by faith. In large measure this present generation of believers has seen one side of faith. It is the side of action, enterprise, and persevering effort, which in the right context is valid and necessary. However, there is an equally necessary expression of faith which results in an entirely different response. It is the activity of waiting or standing.

This posture is appropriate for issues beyond the realm of our actual authority or ability. Many times people have asked me what they should be doing about issues around them. Whether this refers to family, church or business I am inclined to ask the same question: *'What is the realm of your authority?'* Meaning, are you actually in a position of authority in the realm of which you speak. If you do not have the right to act then you must take a more passive role. David understood this! Saul was the King and God had placed him there. It was not in the realm of David's authority to displace Saul. His responsibility was to be upright and faithful within the confines of his present sphere of authority.

In some circles this expression of faith that requires waiting is discouraged. Sometimes this is for good reason. There are many who would substitute mere inactivity for 'waiting on God'. However, equally wrong is the wholesale condemnation of a true faith that waits. A great premium has been set on 'feverish activity', however, at least as much *'Christian service'* is born of fear and unbelief as is born of genuine faith. If our service in the Lord is to be fruitful, it must emerge from confident trust and obedience. Everything else may look as though it produces fruit, but whatever is not born of faith is sin. Actions or enterprises which come from guilt, fear, anxiety or a desire to demonstrate ones worth, zeal or greatness, are simply wasted energy.

Faith is perfected and brought to a place of maturity through the process of the unfulfilled promise over the passing of time. Simply stated, faith is purified through patience. Patience is something that must be exercised over an extended period of time—by nature it cannot be instantaneous. James puts it like this:

"knowing that the testing of your faith produces patience. [4] But let patience have its perfect work, that you may be perfect and complete, lacking nothing." (James 1:3-4)

To which the author of Hebrews adds:

"… that you do not become sluggish, but imitate those who through faith and patience inherit the promises." (Hebrews 6:12)

"And so, after he had patiently endured, he obtained the promise." (Hebrews 6:15)

"For you have need of endurance, so that after you have done the will of God, you may receive the promise: …" (Hebrews 10:36)

This kind of trial or testing of our faith consists of circumstances and situations wherein man has the opportunity to reach, in his own strength and timing, for what God has promised him. The tendency is for man to engage in self-imposed service when immediate success fails to materialize. Samuel had prophesied David's rise to the throne. The test for him was, *'Could he wait for the hand of God to bring to pass what was said, or did David need to bring it about himself?'* The victory is won when one chooses faith over manipulation, charisma or human strength. David's depth of faith is reflected in the fact that even when faced with the chance to destroy the man most responsible for his pain, he waited and refused to devise his own future.

Kingdom Purity

Sometimes we look at the reign of David and wonder how it could be so glorious. We adopt pet phrases such as *"...a man after My own heart, who will do all My will" (Acts 13:22).* But what does it actually mean? What went into the fabric of David's reign that made it what it was?

The glory of David's reign is specifically due to the purity of its roots. The fact that David **waited** for the hand of God is not an insignificant matter. David understood that faith is infused into every initiative. When we build something on behalf of God it is not the outward form or shape that determines what it will be but the posture of our heart when it was birthed.

We often see people mimic the form of someone else's obedience and wonder why the outcomes are not the same. These can be likened to spiritual franchises, and the Church is replete with them. That is, people importing a system from one place to another without the essential components. Faith is an essential but invisible component. For this reason an applied equation will not work in one city the same as in another city. It does not have to be something that complicated. Years ago, I went to the streets of Dallas, Texas to witness. I imagined what it was going to be like and envisioned people being touched, as the very foundations of the Kingdom of Darkness were shaken through the declaration of Christ. When I went out nothing happened; people virtually ignored me and I came away discouraged and dejected. In prayer I cried out to the Lord. I knew that the problem was not Him but I could not understand what went wrong. I had mimicked what others had done, even to the point of using Jesus' very words, but it was not the same.

It is not the sequence of events or the administration details that define an enterprise, it is the essence of the thing at its root. Is it born of God or is it just a really good human attempt and do we even know the difference? Whether that enterprise is an outreach, a church, a family, or a business, the parameters work the same, *"For whatever is born of God overcomes the world. And this is the victory that has overcome the world—our faith" (1 John 5:4).* The durability of a work and the degree of heaven's blessing hinge on the qualities infused at the genesis. For this reason David waited and believed unless sanctioned by authority or instruction. This was a key to the length and breadth of his kingdom. Conveniently, this is the pattern outlined in scripture.

"For whatever is born of God overcomes the world. And this is the victory that has overcome the world—our faith." (1 John 5:4)

"because " All flesh is as grass, and all the glory of man as the flower of the grass. The grass withers, And its flower falls away, but the word of the LORD endures forever." Now this is the word, which by the gospel was preached to you. (1 Peter 1:24-25)

The things that originate from the Word of God have longevity and power which others do not. In David's situation a case could have been made for striking down Saul. No doubt it could have been, and was argued, that God delivered Saul into his hand. After all, should he expect that the throne of Israel would drop into his lap without so much as raising a finger? What is the difference between waiting on God and being passive? How do we know whether our waiting is faith or the absence of courage to act? You cannot know without going through a journey yourself. David took the journey.

The Anatomy of the Journey

David was a man of action before he became a man of patience. This in itself is part of the template of our training. You cannot superimpose another man's example of actual patience onto your own life. The result is mere inactivity!

This reminds me of a story. A young boy came by the shore where sat an elderly grey haired man. He asked the man what he was doing, to which the elder said, "I'm fishing". The young boy plopped down next to him and waited. Before long his brother came along and asked him what he was doing. The boy confidently replied, "I'm fishing". The elder man astutely corrected him by pointing out that he was in fact not fishing but waiting. Fishing required two phases: Action followed by inaction. If you don't put your hook in the water you wait in vain. Fishing appears to be doing nothing but is really a kind of 'active inactivity'. Young believers often make this error in their quest to imitate the faith of an elder saint. The difference is clear in the results.

David's early experiences of faith required a bold stepping into the fray. There he confronts a bear, then a lion and finally Goliath. One would think these are plateaus of ultimate faith but nothing can be further from the truth. The Lord was only beginning David's training. This early faith can influence a moment but it cannot establish and keep a kingdom. It is phase one only! It can win on the field of battle but it cannot restrain the insurrection of the ambitious. The faith required for maintaining a kingdom is more than an occasional interjection of power into a circumstance; it is about unleashing the abilities of God to administrate beyond what we know.

Those who are in the phase of the bear and the lion cannot comprehend such a need. Their perspective is limited to the need for action. When Abishai requests to kill Saul it is because this is the limitation of his faith and understanding. Today many have vacillated between these two expressions without seeing the function or place of either.

When we do not understand the faith behind those who have 'entered His rest' we assume passivity. But you cannot imitate that kind of faith. When you try the outcome is void because there is no actual faith at work. Many have wrongly imitated those who are waiting. This results in a passive 'Calvinist' theology without the mature faith to support it. *The error is not in a mature faith's ability to wait and rest, but in the assumption that waiting and resting equals a mature faith.* The faith-fruit of waiting can only exist if one has been through the growth process.

It evolves out of having stood in faith, with a great deal of human effort, only to find that the human effort was unnecessary. After repeated such ordeals, 'experienced confidence' in God's word results in standing without human effort, which—to the untaught—appears as one doing nothing. In reality, much is being done but the activity has moved from the visible to the invisible. Mature faith is less observable than immature faith because it has moved from the flesh, where it is visible, to the sphere of the Spirit where it is not.

A few years ago one of my associate pastors approached me. I was glad to hear his first statement when he stated having learned something from me. He said, *'when there are problems in the church I come to you, but I know you will do nothing'.* I was unsure of his direction but he continued on to say, *'I know you don't do anything but suddenly everything starts to change'.* He then began to talk about the power of faith in action. There is an invisible administration of the Spirit that can only happen through faith. There is a faith requiring action but faith for governance is something else entirely.

This kind of faith cannot be imitated. Those who try without the benefit of the journey of faith succeed only in embracing a religious behavior void of power. David was able to demonstrate a mature waiting faith because he first graduated from the school of faith. It is not a posture to be imitated, it is a reality forged in the fires of experience. David knew what God required of him because he knew God. He actually believed! Through that belief he was able to unleash the hand of God while at the same time restraining his own. On account of this faith he ensured for himself posterity among the most legendary of Biblical leaders. There is a journey for each of us through similar trial and error. In the end we receive a faith that in turn releases the hand of God, while restraining our own.

9   PRESENT AND FUTURE

What David did as a Leader is obviously important to us.
Perhaps equally critical was the path he took to get there.
Many leaders fail in their journey not because the destination
is wrong, but their journey is incomplete. One of the most
common errors leaders make is the failure to live where they
are rather than where they want to be. David was able to
juggle these two realities without losing sight of either. While
never letting go of the promise to be king, he also succeeded
in remembering he was the youngest of eight brothers.

Youngest of Eight

It must have been tough being last in the company of so many
siblings. There are plenty of opportunities to be measured
and compared. Clearly no one thought much of David. As the
youngest child he must have always been considered that
little 'tag along' older brothers love to get rid of. When
Samuel came to town for a feast, David was not even invited.

He was dismissed out of hand as though he were not even worthy to be considered. (1 Samuel 16:5).

Samuel was distracted by the supremacy of the older sons until one by one; the Lord refuses them. This is where we get the classic line from the Holy Spirit telling us a little of what God is looking for.

"Do not look at his appearance or at his physical stature, because I have refused him. For the Lord does not see as man sees; for man looks at the outward appearance, but the Lord looks at the heart." (1 Samuel 16:7)

The message is clear and simple. God is not impressed by appearances. But this principle was entirely new to both Samuel and the others. David, who had never been considered a man, was sought out (1 Samuel 16:11-12) and eventually anointed. What must this have meant to him? How could he have not relished this moment of vindication as all his brothers were passed over and he was chosen? He must have wanted to bask in the moment remembering all the times he was berated and considered 'marginal'. Everything within him must have wanted to shout out a justification like, "I told you I was important."

His time had come and everyone, including David, knew what it meant to be anointed by the prophet. It was a high honor and at the very least underscored David's ultimate destination: He would be greater than his brothers. The question is 'what would now change?'

Now that an outside authority finally acknowledged him, some special accommodations might be in order. Perhaps he would no longer have to watch the sheep and get a little respect from his brothers. Since the great prophet had anointed him others would begin to bow a little. Nothing changes however! Life goes on exactly as it did before this time.

Later when opportunity calls and Saul asks for David we see he has returned to tending sheep. In fact, his very person seems to have become synonymous with rearing them.

"Therefore Saul sent messengers to Jesse, and said, 'Send me your Son David, who is with the sheep.'"(1 Samuel 16:19)

This is where most would-be-leaders struggle in the journey. Desperately wanting to escape the wilderness of obscurity, we long to fulfill an inner yearning to be effective. When one is called to do great things for God there hovers overhead an impending desire for something different. In this desire is a kind of impatience. This impatience appears to have bonded with the sense of call, but it is altogether something else. The delay can be very strategic in the hand of God. It is part of a sifting process as the Holy Spirit isolates and eliminates the source of the impatience.

When a word comes confirming that sense of destiny we feel, we want to lunge ahead. There is no need to be hasty, as we are in process. Still, it can be confusing. This is primarily because we mistake the promise of a destination as the end, when it is really a beginning. Samuel's prophetic word, like all others speaks to potential and not necessarily to immediate reality. When we receive a prophetic word it is not permission to abandon ship or become the captain. The word is a promise of what we will become if we remain on course.

Our Uniqueness

The impatient man is hungry for recognition and will quickly depart from his proper course. He is quite willing to serve alongside others, until that fateful prophetic word sets him apart. "The prophet said I was an Apostle... a prophet... a person of unique qualities and gifts. Finally I am being recognized for what I always knew." All too often he will depart from the path of simple faithfulness after the smallest amount of recognition or acknowledgment.

This is one of the great dangers of prophetic words. The words might not be wrong but our interpretation of their meaning can put us in extreme peril. So desperate for approval, the slightest amount of attention or commendation suddenly makes us feel superior. Yet, despite our apparent 'special status' we are no different than before we received the word.

This is something David seemed to understand or at least reconciled himself to, because later when Saul sends for him, he is still with the sheep. David's humility enabled him to view the anointing not as acclamation but as a sign of a new beginning. The moment did not signal arrival but declared entry into a new dimension. While it was certainly a privilege for the young man, the anointing did not guarantee success any more than it did for Saul. And we all know how that ended.

There is often an overwhelming need inside us to have the world pay homage to our new status. Part of the purpose of the journey is to kill this self-awareness and it often involves humbling circumstances. At least what seems to be humbling, but in the larger picture is not. It reminds me of a recent sit-com where a bunch of nerdy academics were hanging out. The one with the least amount of qualifications is always being insulted for being low-man on the academic totem pole. Despite the fact he has a master of engineering degree, he is dismissed as being a non-intellectual. Finally, in a fit of desperation and frustration yells, "I have a Masters in Engineering!" Then without so much as a moment's pause, the retort comes back, "Who doesn't?"

The point is this. As much as we want to feel elevated by our uniqueness, we are all very much the same from the perspective of divinity. A significant part of humility is realizing this fact. While our individual achievements might amount to a lot for us personally they are never as unique as they feel. Despite whatever kind of acknowledgement we might receive, in the larger picture we are all just one candidate in a pool of many equally qualified people. These qualifications are not an ending point they are a starting point. When a young man or woman graduates from University with their accreditation as a teacher, dentist or doctor, they are now one of thousands or tens of thousands. Sure, it does signal a kind of belonging that is fresh, but the singular sense of elevation we might feel disappears once we view the vastness of the company we now keep.

Escaping into the Future

Before the Lord can actually elevate us, He must deal with the way we perceive elevation. So long as we are charmed by our new status, we will consider returning to the sheep as something 'beneath us'. The tension we feel in returning to our former affairs is the evidence of superiority. This superiority is an illusion. It is a notion concocted by our own minds to compensate for how we really feel. Whether we realize it or not, in it is a bizarre kind of impulse, whose sole purpose is to help us escape from our present condition. This is false and artificial transformation and will never lead us into our destiny.

Years ago I was forced to come face-to-face with this impulse. Frankly, it was completely hidden from me. The Lord had opened a door to go to Australia after my graduation from Christ for the Nations in Dallas Texas. In my mind I had begun to take the first step toward fulfilling my ministry calling. In reality I was also seeking to escape by becoming someone else. Ministry was now going to be the vehicle of my transformation.

Having received my diploma, I could say goodbye to the old Marc. Not only did I not have to return to my old life, I would not even return to my old country – Canada. After living in Australia for a few months, things were not going well. A series of hardships came upon me. In the midst of the stress God began to show me I might fulfill my calling by returning to Canada and forgetting about ministry. Initially, I was repulsed by the thought. My heart sank as I considered returning to Canada; it spoke of failure and would make my years of education appear misplaced and worthless.

So many of my hopes and dreams were tied into being a pastor or prophet, anything less was intrinsically demoralizing. Finally, the Spirit of God broke through my resistance. One day, I simply and joyfully resigned myself to doing whatever God required, even if it meant returning to construction as a vocation. Knowing I needed to return to Canada I was now prepared to do anything. As God would have it ministry was still His goal. He simply needed to remove from me the sense of diminishment associated with returning. That was also the sense of superiority connected to ministry.

God likewise sent David back to the sheep to test this tension. He was sifting the heart of this young man of all ambition, probing the depths for any hint of superiority. After a small test he was sent to Saul as a minstrel and ultimately an armor-bearer (1 Samuel 16:21). Even so, after all this elevation more tests were in order. Despite his elevation he was still required to tend sheep. The dichotomy must have been heart wrenching, being so close to royalty and power while still having to return to the simplicity of the fields.

"But David occasionally went and returned from Saul to feed his father's sheep at Bethlehem."(1 Samuel 17:15)

This back and forth was a god-kind of exercise designed to create friction. Imagine the difficulty as David was attempting to forge a fresh identity for himself. He has almost solidified his new persona, as a capable up-and-coming-leader, only to be catapulted back to keeper-of-the-sheep. Again and again God would not allow him to use his future to escape the present. In reality, what happens in the hearts of leaders in the making is a 'forging' of a divine sort. Under the pressures of seemingly belittling circumstances, God anchors us to our humanity. Then, while keeping one foot in this reality, He gradually moves us into our destiny. In this fashion elevation is never an escape from reality – it becomes reality. By this way we never lose sight of who we really are in the journey.

The Pull of the Past

These tests continued for David until finally his moment with Goliath was on the horizon. Once again, in obedience to his father he sets course for the battlefield where the Philistines are arrayed against Israel (1 Samuel 17:18). This fateful occasion stirs in him the godly anger destined to define his future. But now another test arises of a different sort.

When David's brother hears of his incendiary remarks over Goliath they are greatly provoked. Perhaps humiliated by his boldness or perceiving rabid ignorance Eliab lashes out. In his mind he still views David as the 'little menace' who ought to be with the sheep. Once again David is assigned the default child status in his brother's eyes. The question is not 'will David's future keep him from the present' but 'will David's past keep him from his future?' At this moment, when he is about to cross the threshold of grace into the anointing for conquest, the voices of his past try to pull him into who he used to be.

"Now Eliab his oldest brother heard when he spoke to the men; and Eliab's anger was aroused against David, and he said, "Why did you come down here? And with whom have you left those few sheep in the wilderness? I know your pride and the insolence of your heart, for you have come down to see the battle." *(1 Samuel 17:28)*

Eliab clearly responds to David's presence, and you can almost feel the stinging with envy from Samuel's previous visit. He wanted to keep the pecking order as it was and put David in his place – the subservient junior. However, this was David's potential moment of transition into his future. It is an evaluation to see if the insecurities of youth remained. If he did not pass the test he would relapse into the past – the youngest of eight and still a little boy. These are the moments we each face. They are designed to evaluate our actual transformation. They are windows of opportunity which, when they come they reveal your mettle; there is no anticipation or posturing that can get you by. Eliab's words pierced like a pitchfork probing and looking to skewer a little boy.

Like every sibling, David's brothers knew how to subdue each other. Rivalries such as these can extend and influence far into our adult years - familiar words hoping for predictable responses. Would the words of Eliab evoke a paralyzing emotional response in David or had he actually grown past them? Of course, we know the legendary end. David is the victor in more ways than one. He has successfully navigated from promise into destiny having finally arrived at his destination. The destination is not his position as king, but the actual change of his nature through the process of walking out the calling. His position and nature have become congruent – they agree with one another.

The Bible tells us, "many are called while few are chosen". (Matthew 20:16) There is a very good reason for this. A man or woman who is called by God is like someone invited to train for a vocation. There are no guarantees of making the grade. Opportunity does not automatically suggest arrival. While Samuel anointed David to be king there remained a great many tests and trials to endure. Like each of us, there remains a long and arduous journey. Completing the journey is not a matter of a mere promise, but of humility, patience and faith. We must guard against the presumption so often found in us reminding ourselves of the words of the king of Israel. When responding to a boast he replied, *"Let not the one who puts on his armor boast like the one who takes it off "*. (1 Kings 20:11) Now those are words to live by.

10   LEADERSHIP – A GIFT

Leadership is a gift that comes out of God encounters. While behaviors, principles and styles of leadership can be learned and imitated, they fall short of true leadership.

Unfortunately, far too often what we see is the pursuit of an 'image of leadership', rather than the actual thing. There is a vast difference between leading and projecting an image of a leader. Sadly, many never come to this understanding. Image worship is the natural consequence. As a result, today we find ourselves in a leadership vacuum. Like the shallow efforts young teenage men make towards manhood, 'pretend leaders' are equally obvious. It does not need to be this way. God in His wisdom has a training program beyond all measure.

Authenticity

Some of the differences are easily illustrated. For example six men came to a party where they were challenged to dress, act and speak like Jamaicans. The end of the evening would require a vote as to which one was most authentic. One of them had an advantage–he *was* Jamaican. The others applied makeup, practiced their accents and donned 'Rastafarian wigs'. For fear of having makeup rub off, they could not move, hug or be touched while guarding their façade. The genuine on the other had no such limitations. Consequently he was at ease as he simply needed to be himself. This kind of reality is at the heart of true leadership.

David exemplified for us the classic great leader. He was neither a pretender nor fabricator of any kind. This air of legitimate authenticity is likely the most coveted facet of his legacy. Authenticity is a hard thing to fake. Everyone wants to be authentic but few can afford to be as the impatience of ambition will not allow it. The results of impatience are not only less than what they promise, they can be devastating. Let me be clear! God is in the business of creating genuine leaders and not shallow empty carbon copies. These are mere images.

Images, like statues, are cold, lifeless and rigid. They are by their very nature unreal and unbending, unwilling and unable to do what needs to be done to lead. They posture themselves continuously to find the most popular side of every matter. Because they are lifeless and unreal, they portray a form of the thing they wish to be, but lack the humanity. Robotically they spout prescribed responses, sometimes even with a clever sincerity. They memorize and practice the posture of the resolute and decisive.

Everything is an act, a fascinating role where life is a stage and 'being real' is a flawed premise share by only the naïve and powerless. At the heart of this philosophy is an insidious and malicious quest for supremacy that is at best incredibly temporary. Nevertheless it empowers a disposition always mindful of appearance. These unbending creatures betray an underlying fear and great insecurity. The goal of their existence, if it is not the case at the outset, becomes mere self-preservation. Every accomplishment amplifies this need, and over time, it gives way to reckless cruelty. Anything but exposure is the primary goal. The higher the stakes or greater the status, the more feverish will be man's attempts to conceal the truth. David, on the other hand, embodied humility; unafraid to look in the mirror of reality.

Very early in my journey God gave me a wakeup call and if memory serves me well, there have been many down through the years. This one however is definitive in as much as it is embarrassing. I had been a Christian for some years and was in the early phase of 'walking out my calling'. To be honest I was stumbling in the dark without a clue.

There seemed a pattern for ministries like mine which included speaking at churches wherever I could. I was calling people and pastors I knew in order to secure invitations. One such man had been a close family friend who lived in the United States. I gave him a call in the hopes he would invite me down for a weekend of ministry. As I spoke to him, I was unaware I had put on a 'professional air/image', as though introducing myself to a stranger. He was baffled and I could hear his confusion. Interrupting my blather he asked, *'Is this Marc Brisebois... like... the one that I know?'*

Suddenly I felt totally embarrassed and exposed as though someone had ripped the covers off of my naked body. Stumbling with some lame apology for my approach, I vainly attempted to recover or restart the conversation.

This moment was an exposure. It enabled me to see my own attempts to sound and look authoritative and convincing. God used it to show me the image I was tending. This kind of exposure is typical if we hope to obtain the kind of reality David had in his journey.

Whether we realize it or not there are two very different plains on which life is being played out. There are those things God is building and conversely, those things man is building. The one cannot compare to the other. What God builds into man is permanent. It has a resolute strength that is far more penetrating and convincing than anything man can clothe himself with. We are always faced with a choice; to take the shortcut promising the illusion of leadership or we can actually become leaders. David chose intimacy with Jonathan, restoration with Abner, endured conflict while walking with Joab, embraced discipline through Shimei, and expressed patience and faith in his ordeal with Saul. While he made mistakes the clear direction of his heart was to please God and grow in an authentic and humble manner.

The choice to forsake the ways of God will require a talent for pretense and deception, and will yield ever-increasing fear and confusion. The alternative is beautiful on all accounts. It allows a person the sanctity and refuge found only in authenticity then, like David, they are free to venture and fail.

Faith secures their destiny and allows the person to live a life rooted in the knowledge of God. This is the kind of leadership the world needs today. It is also the kind God is recruiting for placement in His very own administration—a Kingdom without end.

The Life of David and his rise ascension into eternal history is a tale of incredible proportions. These five stones are five living monuments cemented together by an understanding worth the weight of the world in gold. They point to vital and timeless principles that are not locked away in an archived museum as testimony of a distant past. They remain relevant, personal and present for anyone wishing their existence to matter beyond the length of their days.

ABOUT THE AUTHOR

Marc Brisebois is husband to Wendy and the father of five children. Rich in ministry experience, he has been a feature on the landscape of the Church in Canada for the last 20 years. Watchman on the Wall Ministries, which was founded by Marc Brisebois, has operated in Canada since 1989. It is a proven ministry and has, over the years, developed a righteous standard for the Body of Christ.

Marc speaks with a prophetic & apostolic voice to this generation and has a passion to teach believers to know how to hear the voice of God for themselves and grow into Christ-likeness. Marc is the senior leader at Spruce Grove Community Church, where he is helping people walk out their gifting through foundational teaching & practical ministry.

Watchman on the Wall Ministries has participated in developing the believing community in over 35 Nations. Marc travels extensively while also being a part of the Canadian Prophetic Council.

WATCHMAN ON THE WALL - RESOURCE INFORMATION

If you have enjoyed reading this book, you will enjoy the number of CDs & DVDs available from Marc Brisebois & Watchman on the Wall Ministries.

Watchman on the Wall also produces a television program called 'Off the Wall', airing on two different networks across Canada.   These can be viewed on the Watchman website

Resources can be viewed & purchased online at:
www.watchman.ca

You can also go to the website and enjoy some of the great articles Marc has written over the years. These are timely and relevant as you walk out your own journey with the Lord.

Watch for Marc's next book release "Real Climate Change" in early 2012.

WATCHMAN ON THE WALL MINISTRIES

www.watchman.ca

MINISTRY CONTACT:

Box 3458
180 Century Road
Spruce Grove, AB. T7X 3A7
CANADA

780.962.5699

info@watchman.ca